MY GLOUCESTER

All good wishes to you!
Marion O'Connell Frost
aka Mimi

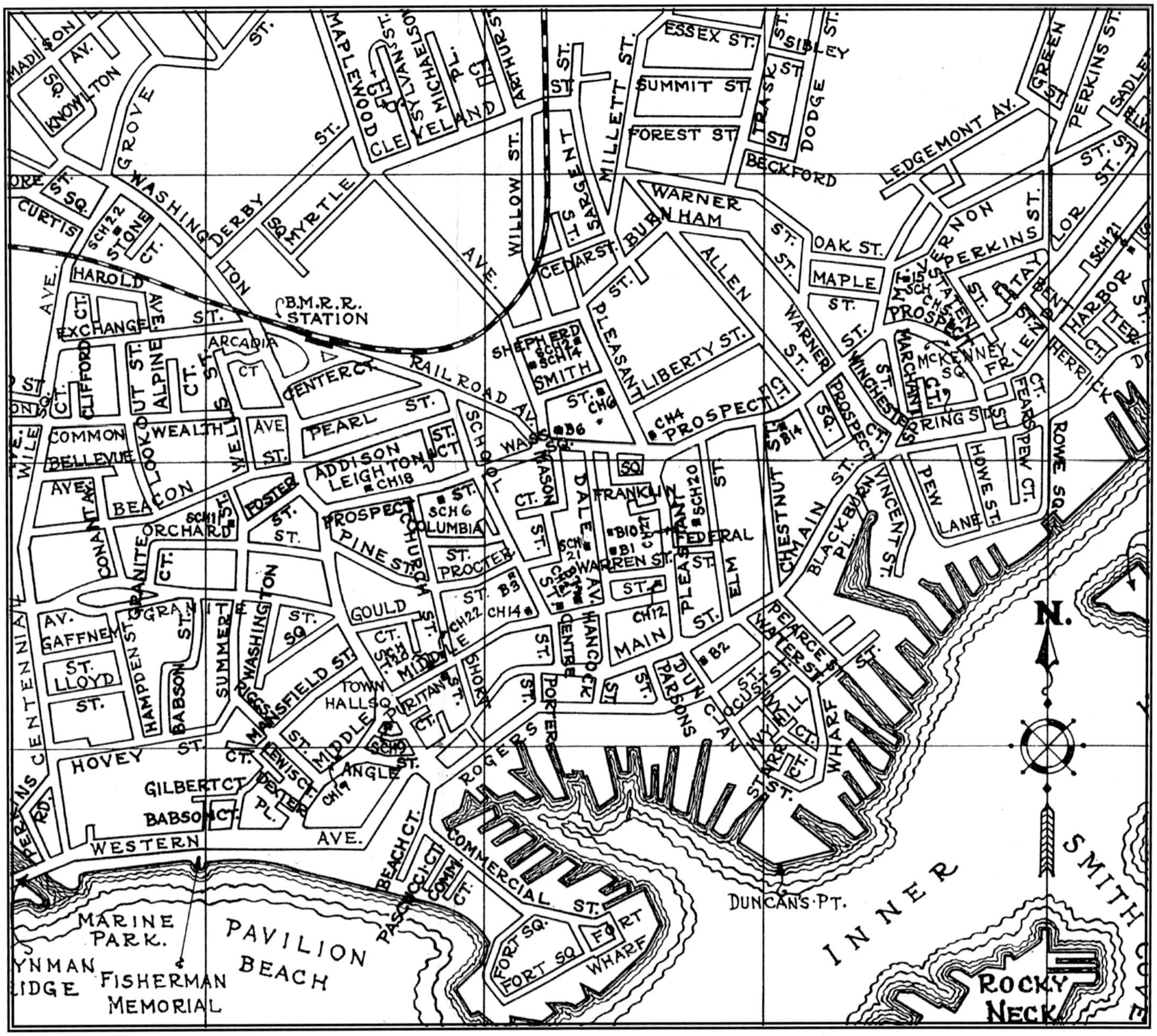

Downtown Gloucester before Urban Renewal, Lucas Map 1947, Courtesy of Cape Ann Museum

MY GLOUCESTER

Views of a Provincial

Marion O'Connell Frost

BRIER NECK PRESS
Gloucester, Massachusetts

This book is dedicated
to my parents, John B. and Celia E. O'Connell,
and to the city of Gloucester.

Cover and interior design by Judith Arisman
Typesetting and layout by Judith Arisman
Edited by Jennifer Ray

Printed by King Printing. Lowell, Massachusetts.
All photographs are original and the work of the author. Skylight filters were the only filters used.

ISBN 0-9841294-6-4

Front Cover: Brace Cove.
Frontispiece: 1947 Lucas map courtesy of Cape Ann Museum, Gloucester, Massachusetts.
Back Cover: Fisherman's Shack, Lane's Cove.

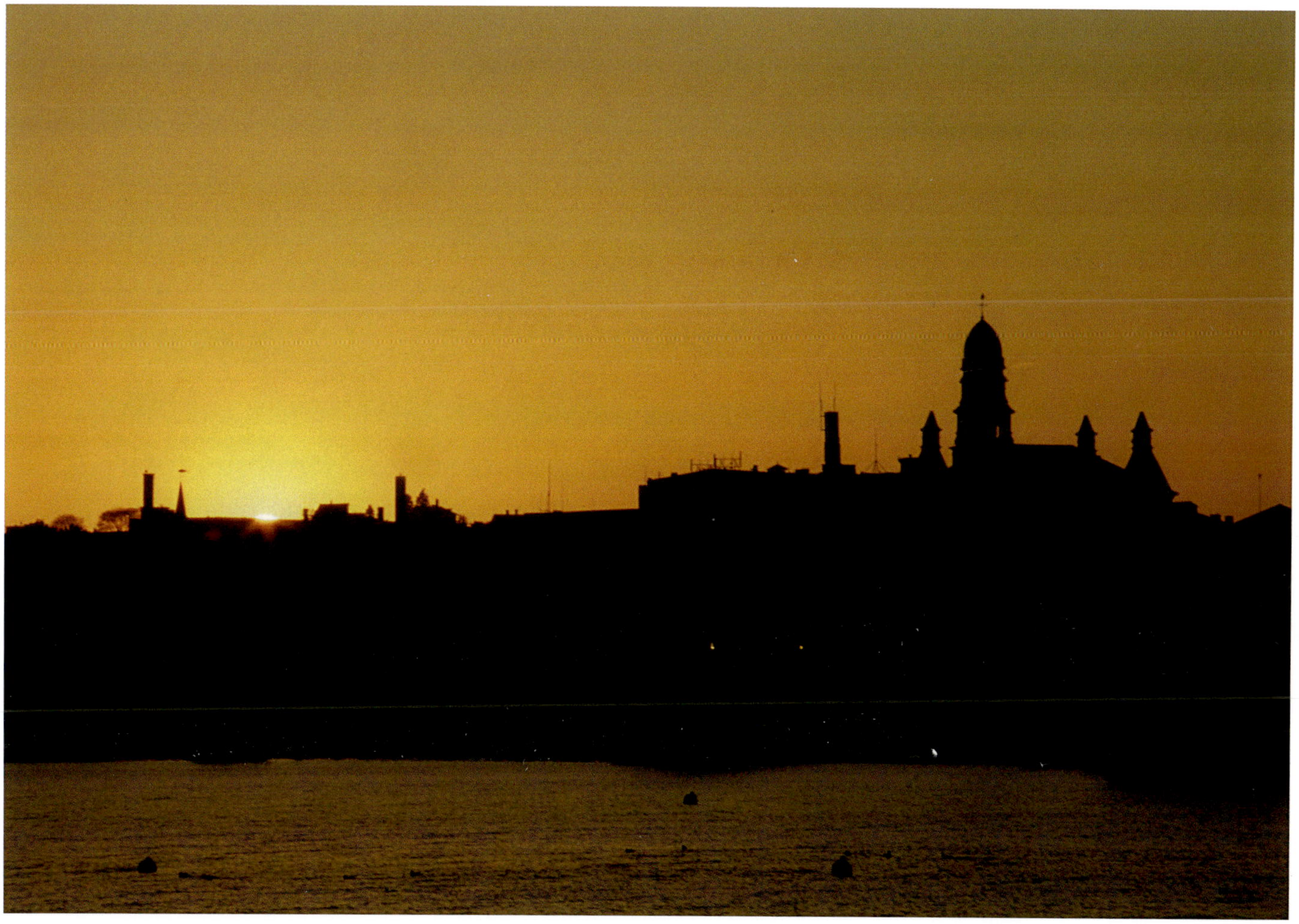

Sunset from the Fish Pier

Preface

When I rented a cottage in Lane's Cove in the fall of 2004 for a week, I didn't plan to write a book. My intention was simply to enjoy being in Gloucester, my hometown. I wanted to visit my favorite areas during the day and early evening and not be concerned about a twenty-minute drive to Ipswich, where I've lived for over forty years. More than anything, I wanted to sleep in Gloucester; I wanted to wake up in Gloucester.

I did take my camera gear with me, sure that I'd take at least a few pictures. I thought I might work on a short photographic essay. That was the extent of my plans.

So after moving in on Saturday, I set out on Sunday, September 4, 2004. My first stop was Pavilion Beach at the eastern end of the boulevard. I sat on one of the benches for a while. I looked; I listened; I breathed in the salt air. I felt at home.

Then I focused on the small beach close to the Tavern wall where my mother, younger sister, Margie, and I used to come, back in the 1930s. We'd often walk here from home on a summer's day. As I studied the beach with its seaweed, trash and rounded rocks I could see that it hadn't changed. To my eyes, it was the same magical, beautiful place!

While photographing the beach, an idea came to me suddenly! I could photograph some of my favorite places in Gloucester and write about childhood memories that reflected the photographs. This beach was a perfect example. Yes! I was going to do this. During the rest of the day, the idea continued to expand. As I was making a mental list of places significant to me, childhood memories were flooding my mind.

That evening, back in my cottage, I knew exactly what I was going to do. I was going to write a full-length book. It would be unique, as no one had yet done what I planned to do. It would contain carefully composed photographs complemented by nostalgic text that would reflect the 1930s and 1940s when I was growing up in the city.

I slept very little that night or any night for the rest of the week. I was as excited as I've ever been in my life! I knew that this project would require much planning and effort, but I looked forward to my photographic visits to Gloucester. For me, they would be a pleasure. I also looked forward to telling my stories. The writing would not be easy, but I knew I could do it. There was much work ahead, but I was ready!

Introduction

Ask anyone who grew up in Gloucester during the '30s and the '40s, as I did, if it wasn't a beautiful time and place to grow up in, and they'll invariably give you an emphatic "Yes!" Looking back, it's easy to see why.

We lived on what is essentially an island. At the end of the line we were somewhat isolated. I think this made us more independent and reflective. There was no television, just radio. We were not bombarded with news and advertisements. Our lives were rather narrow when we were small children. We had our neighborhoods and then our neighborhood schools. Most of us walked everywhere all year round. We walked downtown, to the library, to shops and to the movies. We walked to and from school twice a day. For the most part, our mothers were at home, but they didn't drive us around. There were few two-car families. Many families had no car. But what we had was freedom. We made up our own games, whether it was softball or jump rope. Adult supervision was minimal. No one worried about us. There didn't seem to be any reason to worry. The pace was slow; life was safe.

I'll admit that some things have changed in Gloucester. The streets are crowded with noisy cars and trucks, often with radios blaring. Grant Circle is backed up twice a day with commuters. The inner harbor is no longer filled with fishing boats; the wharves are not bustling with fish processing. Main Street has lost many of its fine shops. Housing is expensive and condos are increasingly popular.

But the essence of the city remains. When I'm here, it's as if I've never been away. I visit my favorite spots—the beaches, the boulevard, the City Lot, Lanesville and the Cove, Rocky Neck—and I'm smiling. Sometimes, tears come to my eyes because it's all so beautiful…the boulevard at sunrise, the wharves in fog, Rocky Neck in the winter. Everything about this place makes me feel at home.

It's not only the sights, though. It's many other things. The topography, for instance. I like all of the ledges, boulders and rocks. I like the marshes, too. And then there are the sounds—surf pounding and seagulls mewing—and of course the smells—low tide, old fish and diesel fuel near the wharves, the salt air coming in on an east wind and the strong odor of fish sticks from Gorton's. All of these things make me feel at home, but more important than any of them is the people. Yes, the people. The people haven't changed. Everywhere I go, I hear welcoming words. They encourage me with my photography. "Good luck" or "I'll bet you got a good one that time." They give me help when I need it, too. As I was driving unknowingly the wrong way on a side street, a woman stopped me and said, "This is a one way street. Go down there to the right and you'll be OK." Thank you, lady!

Sometimes I wonder if I find Gloucester one of the most beautiful places in the world because I was born and brought up here. So many locations speak to me of happy and beautiful moments from the past, whether it's a wild winter storm on the Back Shore, late afternoon light falling on my mother's garden on Beacon Street, or sunrise as seen from the City Lot, each place has its special memories.

Then, I think about other places where I've lived and the many countries I've visited all around the world. I've seen beauty everywhere. I've been awed by the alpen glow of the Himalayas, sunrise on the Ganges, the intense blue of the icebergs in Antarctica and much more. But always, as beautiful and exciting as these places and sights have been, I've thought that none of them is more beautiful than Gloucester.

Yes, I have benefited in many ways from traveling, for instance in cultural enrichment and in the understanding of geography. I am truly grateful to have been so privileged; I thank my late husband, Dave, especially. But now, as I'm growing older, I find that not only is travel more difficult for me, but also that my wanderlust is diminishing! What I want now is to focus on what is close by and, in my mind, the very best place of all—Gloucester. Or, as my Dad would say, "the fair city of Gloucester."

Friendly Marshes–1942

My mother: "Girls, how about walking to Riverdale this afternoon?" It was a warm Sunday afternoon early in the fall. Our answer: "OK!" A walk from Beacon Street to Riverdale where Great Aunt Nan, Great Uncle Homer and Aunt Marion lived was about a forty-minute walk.

Part way there we came to this marshy area. Back in the '40s before Route 128 was built, the Ellery House was located on the western side of Washington Street, where part of Grant Circle is now. There were a few small trees and a garden near the house. Beyond the garden were the marshes.

Every time I passed this area I surveyed the marshes, watching them turn color from yellow-green in the spring to tawny gold in the fall. Sometimes in a hard winter they'd be covered with ice that glistened in the sunshine.

Years later after Route 128 was built, I'd drive my mother to the Friendly's parking lot near the former location of the Ellery House. Enjoying our ice cream cones as we faced the marshes and the highway, we would note the wildlife in this mini-sanctuary and admire the ever-changing beauty of the marshes. It was a favorite spot in Gloucester for us both. It still is for me.

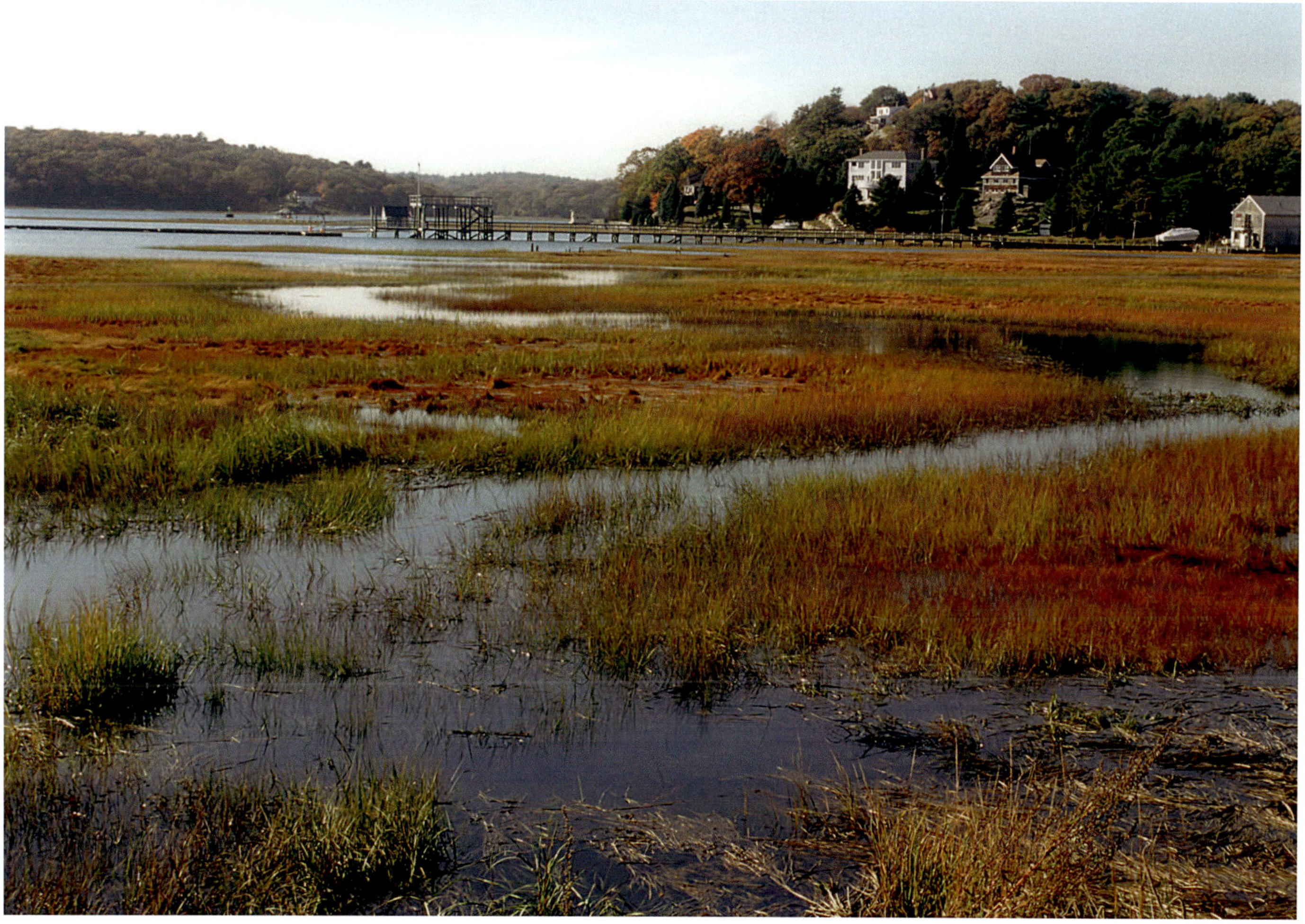

The City Lot

Living on Beacon Street, I played on Governor's Hill, or as we all knew it, the City Lot. Behind my house and up a rocky incline, it was then a rough place with lots of ledges and wild grapes near the summit, and much poison ivy along the Beacon Street boundary. My younger sister Margie, the little rascal, deliberately rubbed the leaves all over her hands one summer so she wouldn't have to wash the supper dishes!

The view of the city was panoramic. My Dad, who owned O'Connell's Variety Store at 89 Washington Street, always advised his customers, looking for a choice view, to go up to the City Lot. From here they would see the outer harbor, the breakwater, Ten Pound Island and the humming city itself with church steeples projecting skyward and City Hall clock tower with its clock telling the correct time. There was no excuse for being late for supper!

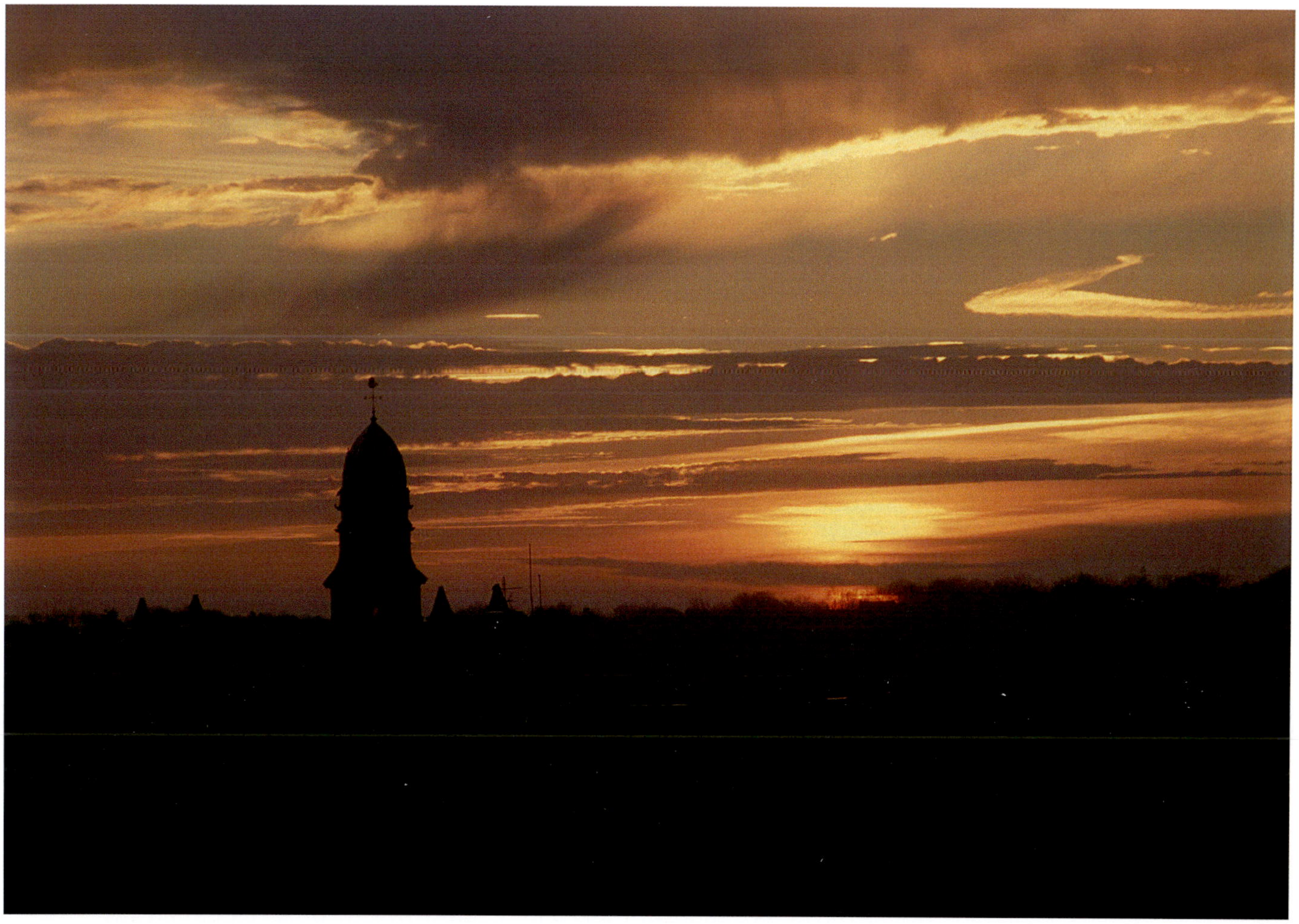

Good Harbor Beach—1930s

I looked forward to Thursday afternoons especially during the summer. My Aunt Marion had the afternoon off from her job as the bookkeeper at the Addison Gilbert Hospital. A sunny day meant Good Harbor Beach for us! Great Uncle Homer would drive Aunt Marion downtown from Riverdale, pick up my mother, my sister and me and away we'd go. Always to the Brier Neck end, of course. I had the impression, probably from adult talk, that Brier Neck was the more choice area. After Uncle Homer dropped us off, we'd trudge through the squeaky hot sand until we found a suitable spot. Quickly, Aunt Marion and my mother would set up the green and orange striped beach umbrella. What a time! Sun and shade, water and sand and, if we were lucky, the breakers would be huge!

Now, when I'm walking the beach I often find myself singing a song I learned in the fifth grade at the old Collins School where MacPherson Housing is now located: "Galloping in with the evening tide, horses stride, horses stride..."

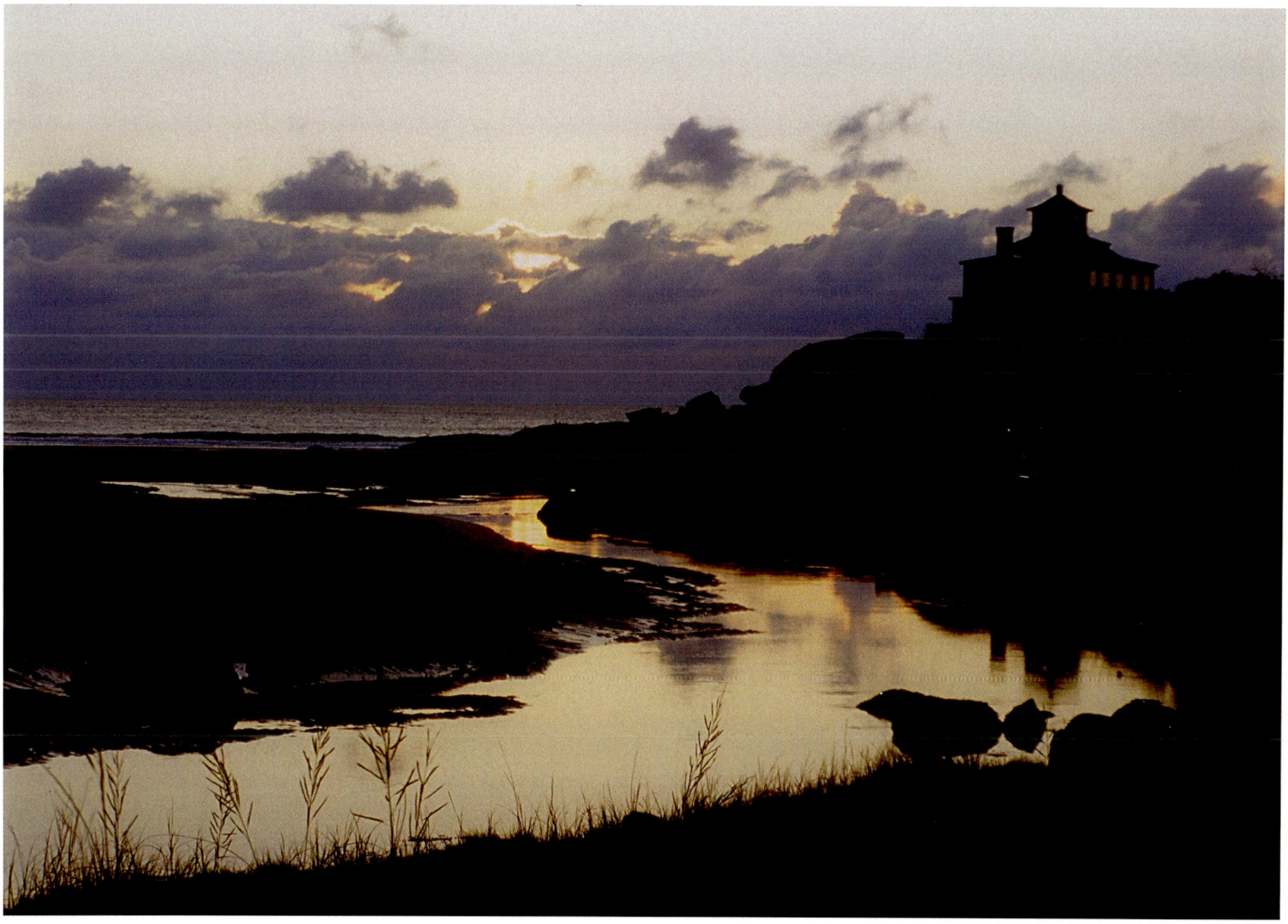

Magnolia Tree–1937

"Look at all those clam shells!" I innocently exclaimed. My family laughed at my ignorance. I was eight then and had never seen a magnolia tree in bloom. I had never seen magnolia blossoms on the ground, either. They looked to me just like the clamshells Uncle Homer spread on his driveway in Riverdale, clamshells he crushed gradually as he drove over them in his car. But these weren't clamshells. They were magnolia blossoms beneath the tree in the side yard of our new home.

I treasure the memory of that day and eagerly watch every year for the brief show of the magnolias, like this one in Annisquam.

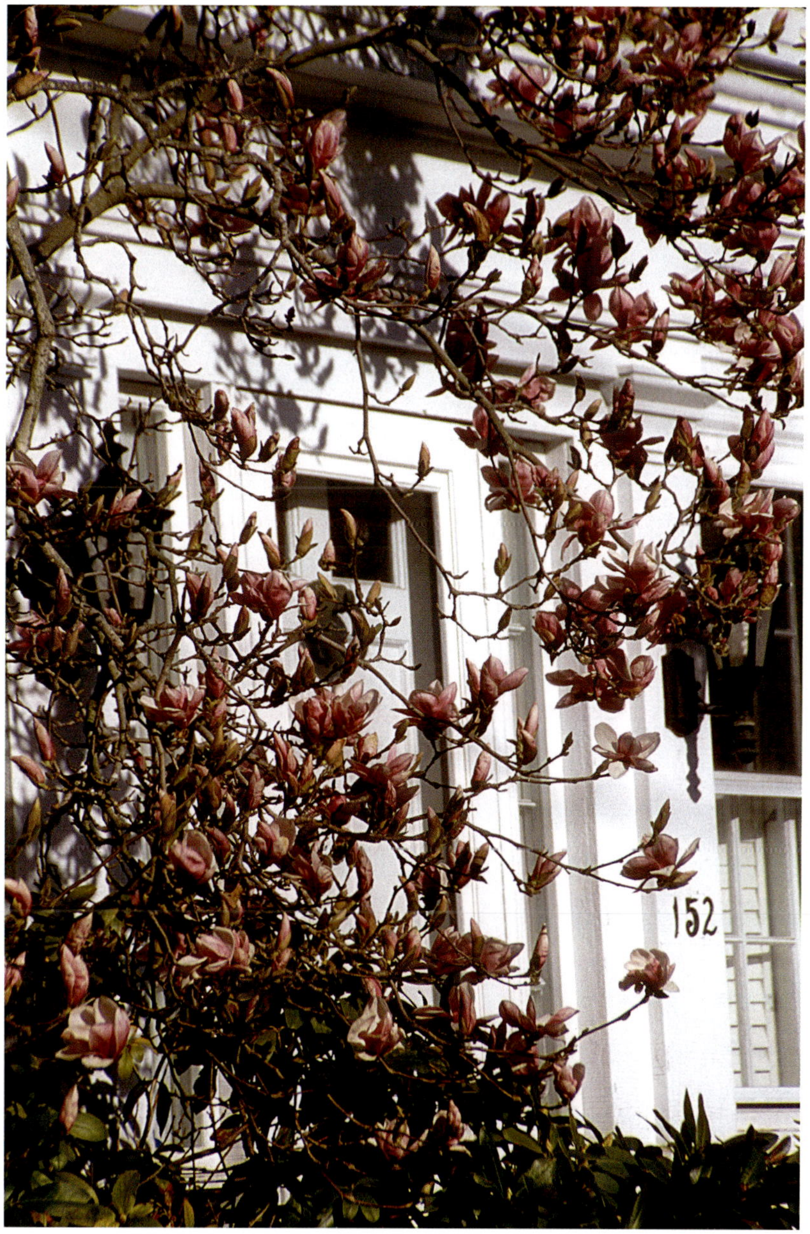
152

Bus Ride to Plum Cove Beach–1937

Here comes the bus! The gray and white Lanesville and Folly Cove bus. My mother, younger sister Margie and I climb aboard. My mother, who surely knows everyone in Gloucester, greets the driver, "Gink" Reed, in her usual friendly way, inquiring after his family.

Then off we go for a summer vacation day at Plum Cove Beach, at the back of the Cape. It's a perfect day! Sunny and warm, blue skies and puffy fair weather clouds. We pass familiar landmarks—the hospital, the Mill Pond and Riverdale—and soon we're in the shade of the Annisquam willows where it's cool and rather dark. Next we drive along a causeway, with a sparkling view of Ipswich Bay and many sailboats moored near the Annisquam Yacht Club. Up the hill, around several curves and we pass Bay View where Aunt Anna and Uncle Skib live. One more hill and we're there!

The beach at Plum Cove is relatively small. We're lucky then that the tide is going, giving us more space. It's a clean beach with fine, white sand. Margie and I dig and make sand castles. We paddle around in the water to cool off. It's a memorable day.

Across Ipswich Bay is the town of Ipswich where I live now. I often look across the bay to Gloucester and think about the days I spent at Plum Cove Beach.

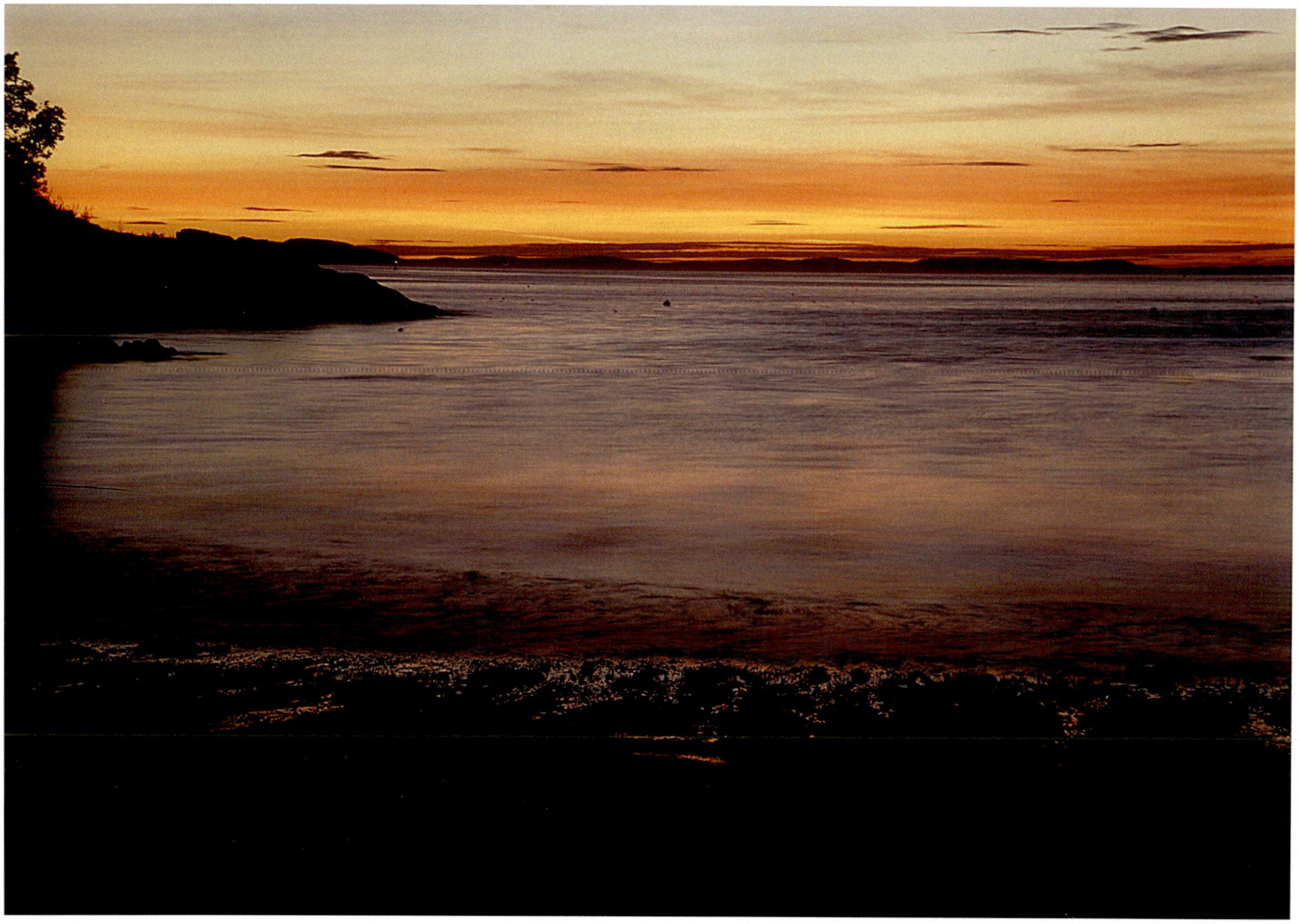

Hovey School Steps–September 1937

My mother: "Where's Margie? It's time for breakfast." Then to me, "Mim, go find your sister. She must've gone outdoors."

Out I went. Not in our yard, not in neighbors' yards. She was nowhere to be seen. Where could she be? I had an idea! Quickly I ran down the hill. A couple of minutes later, I did a right turn onto Summer Street and there was the Hovey School where I'd be in third grade this year. And guess who was sitting on the steps? Margie, a lively, enthusiastic kid about to start school—the next day.

"Come on home," I said. "School doesn't start until tomorrow." "Tomorrow? What do you mean, tomorrow?" Margie said with great disappointment, "I want to go today!" Reluctantly, she followed me up the hill. Would the first day of school never come?

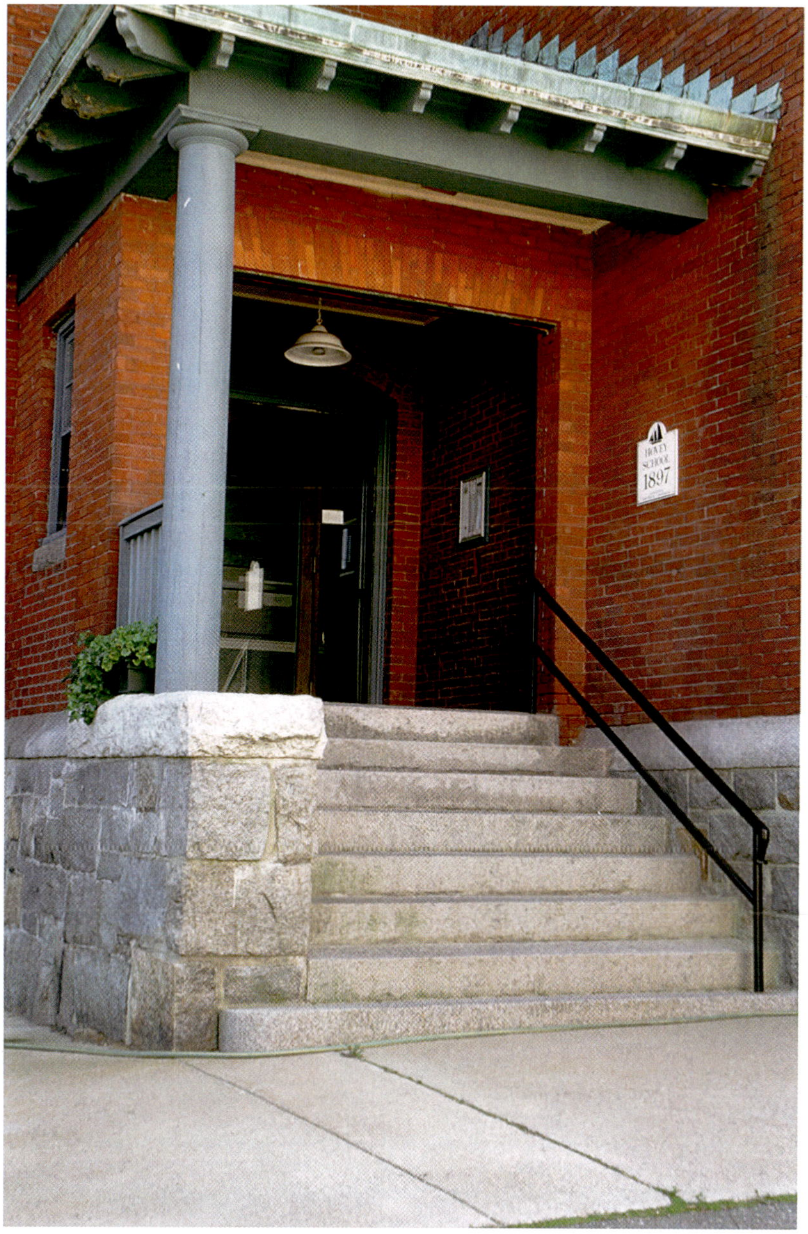
HOVEY
SCHOOL
1897

Young Girl with Pomegranate–1938

What is that curly haired girl eating? I wondered. Passing her on my way to afternoon session at the Hovey School, one warm fall day, I could see an apple-like object in her left hand. With the stained fingers of her right hand she was picking out red seeds that she popped into her mouth. How I wanted to taste some of those seeds! But I didn't know this kid. I couldn't ask her to share with me.

A while later I discovered, in a local fruit store, what she'd been eating. A pomegranate! (Back then that was a foreign fruit.) So it was some time later before I bought one. What messy fun to eat! As I was savoring the slightly tart seeds, I was picturing that cute, curly haired girl and wishing I hadn't waited so long.

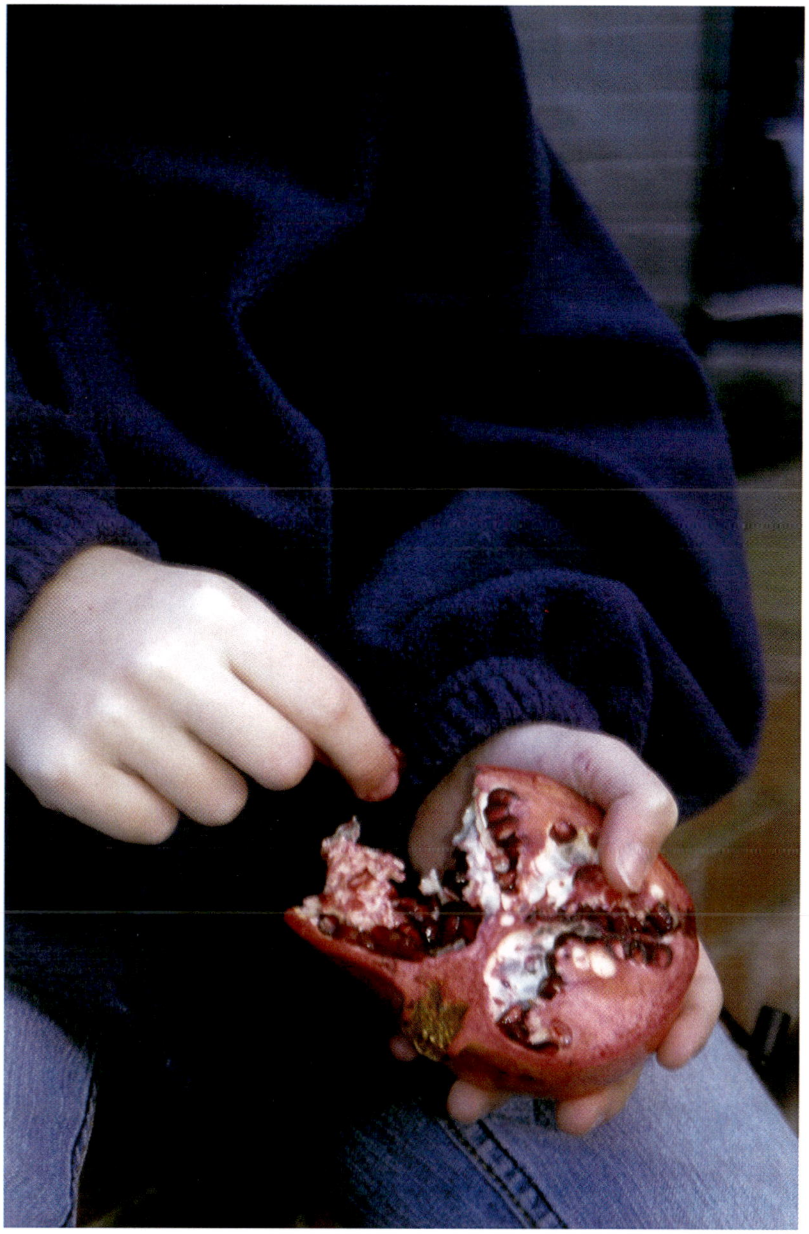

Carillon Concerts

Smell those fish sticks! As I'm standing on an outcrop in Ledgemont Park, I'm looking down on the workaday city. It's a hazy, early spring morning and the smell of Gorton's is strong up here. But good! Close by are the towers of Our Lady of Good Voyage Church. I can see clearly the carillon in the nearer tower. For three years now the bells, needing repair, have been silent, but I well remember the pealing of the bells on Sunday mornings and the summer concerts during my childhood. On Wednesday evenings the music would carry all the way across the city to my home on Beacon Street! I would stop whatever I was doing and listen with delight.

As soon as the carillon is repaired, and the concerts are given again, I'll drive to Governor's Hill in Gloucester. I'll climb the short distance to the summit where I'll be able to see the towers. Then I'll listen to the music as it floats in waves across the city. Just as I did when I was a kid.

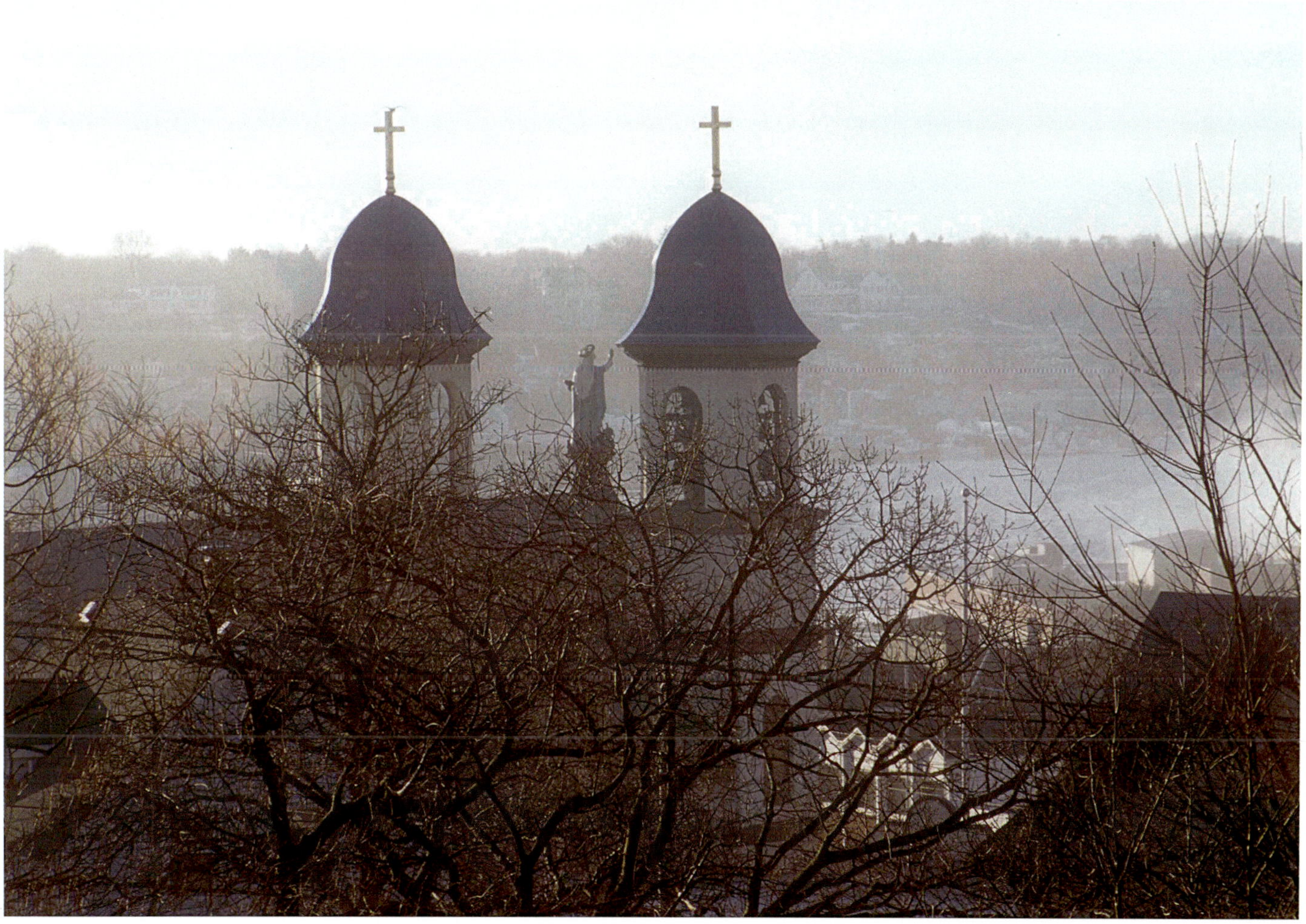

Brace Cove–1940s

During the early 1940s when my Great Uncle Homer delivered our weekly quart of clams—clams he had dug and shucked—I sometimes went along for the ride as he finished his route. One fall afternoon when the wooden box containing the jars of clams was empty, Uncle Homer suggested a ride around the Back Shore. It was getting close to sunset. As we approached the sharp right turn from Atlantic Avenue onto Farrington Avenue, Uncle Homer slowed the car down, giving us a brief but clear view to our left of Brace Cove and the rock. Beautiful! I think he liked this spot as much as I did!

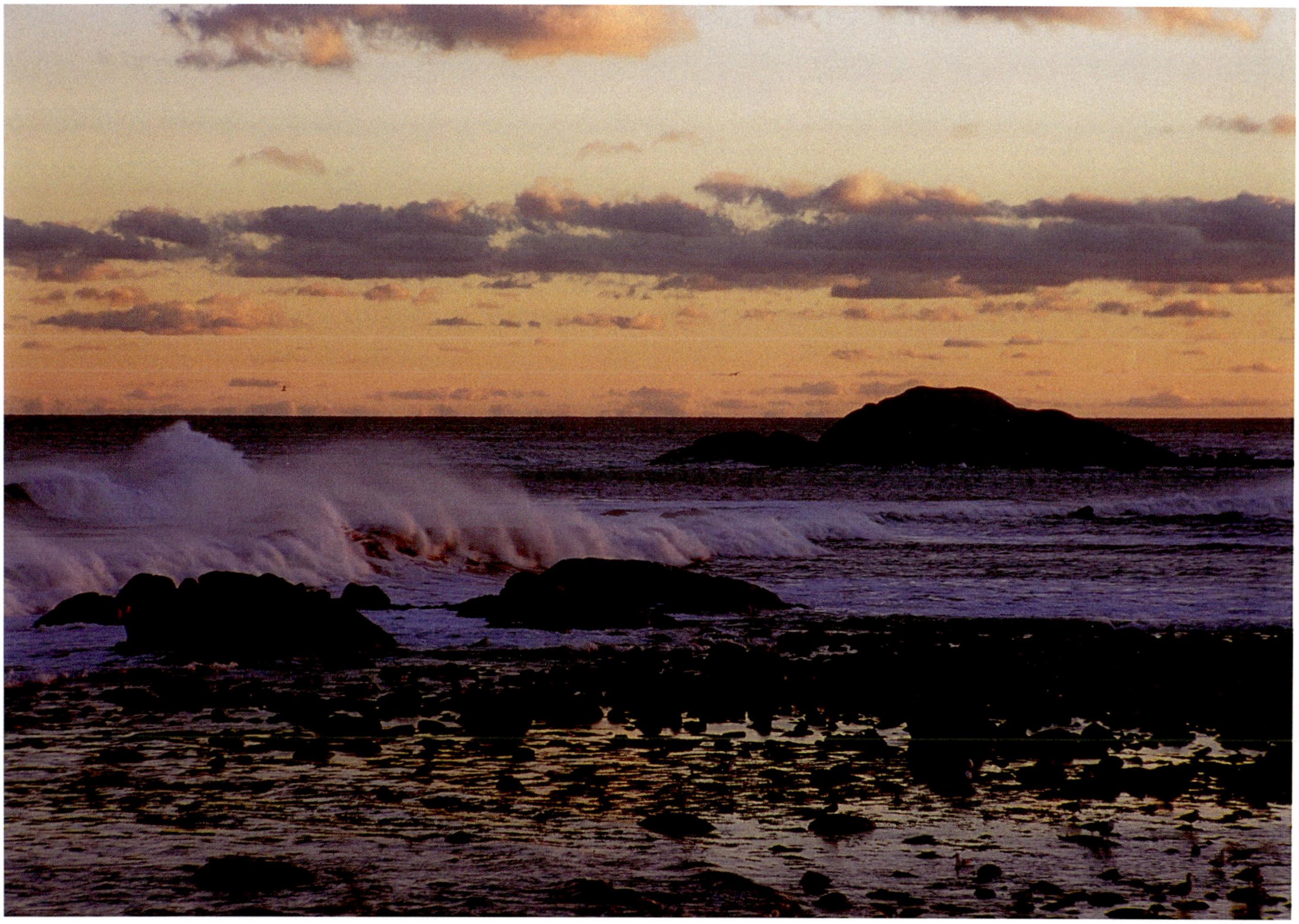

City Hall Clock from Duncan Street

From most parts of the city you can catch a glimpse of this clock tower.
As a kid I was grateful to be able to see it. Not having a watch,
I counted on being able to see the clock so I'd be on time for school.
In those days we all went home for lunch. Twice a day for three
years I walked the fifteen minutes back and forth to Central Grammar.
I prided myself on not ever being marked "tardy" on my report card.

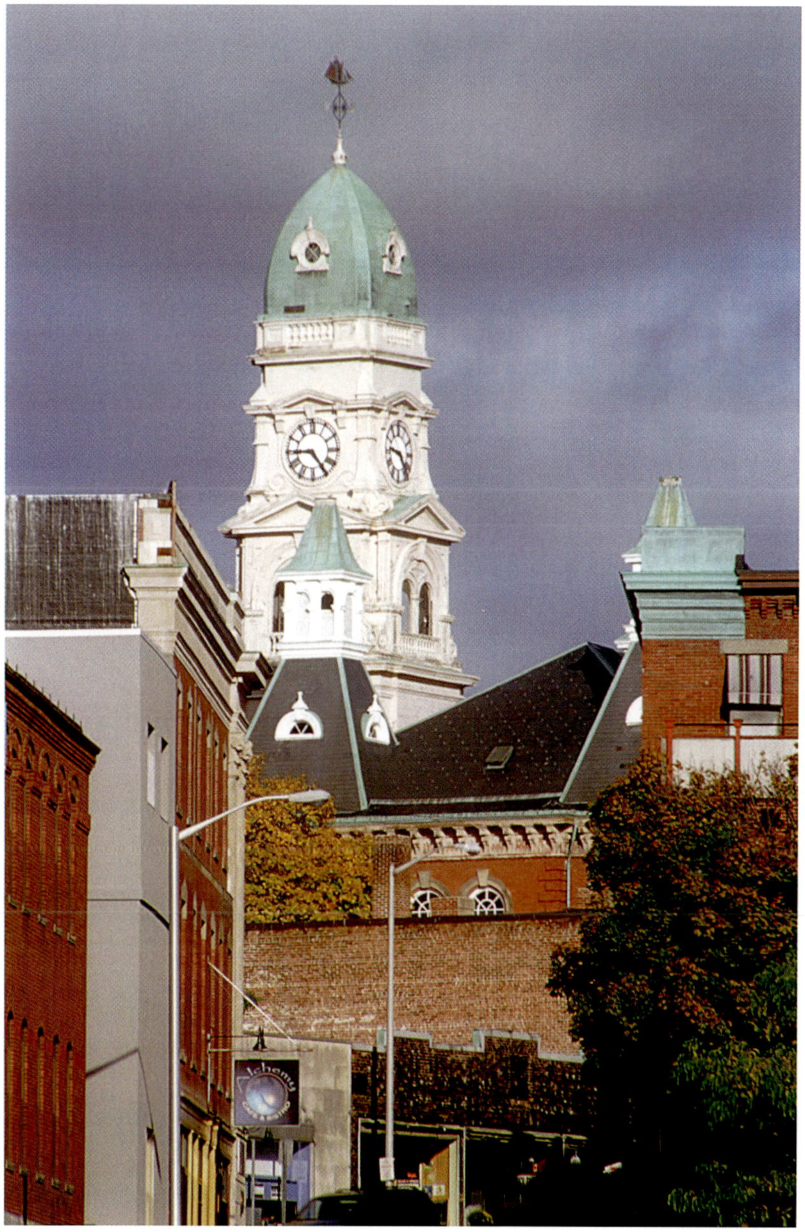

Ten Pound Island from Ledgemont Park

Seeing the late afternoon light on Ten Pound Island on a cool sunny day in April, I was thinking that it could be April 1941. It's spring vacation week and my whole sixth grade class at Central Grammar has been invited to spend the day on Ten Pound Island by a classmate, Ed Hopkins. His father is the lighthouse keeper and Ed and his family live out there.

Early in the morning, we all meet Ed at the town landing on Commercial Street. He's twelve years old, and yes, he's operating the boat, *Peggy Anne*, a gill netter he's borrowed from a friend. No one questions this. Ed is a capable captain and quickly takes us to the island.

The rest of the day is spent touring the lighthouse, eating lunch and hanging around with our friends. Of course, we did enjoy watching a certain girl as she flirted with several boys! Just before we left the island, someone took a picture of the class and our teacher, Miss Johnson. I smile every time I look at that picture, remembering our great adventure.

Now, many years later, I sometimes pretend I'm in my bed at home on Beacon Street. It's a foggy night, the air is damp, the sheets are clammy and I hear the bell on Ten Pound Island. Ding, ding… ding, ding…every three or four seconds. Ding, ding.

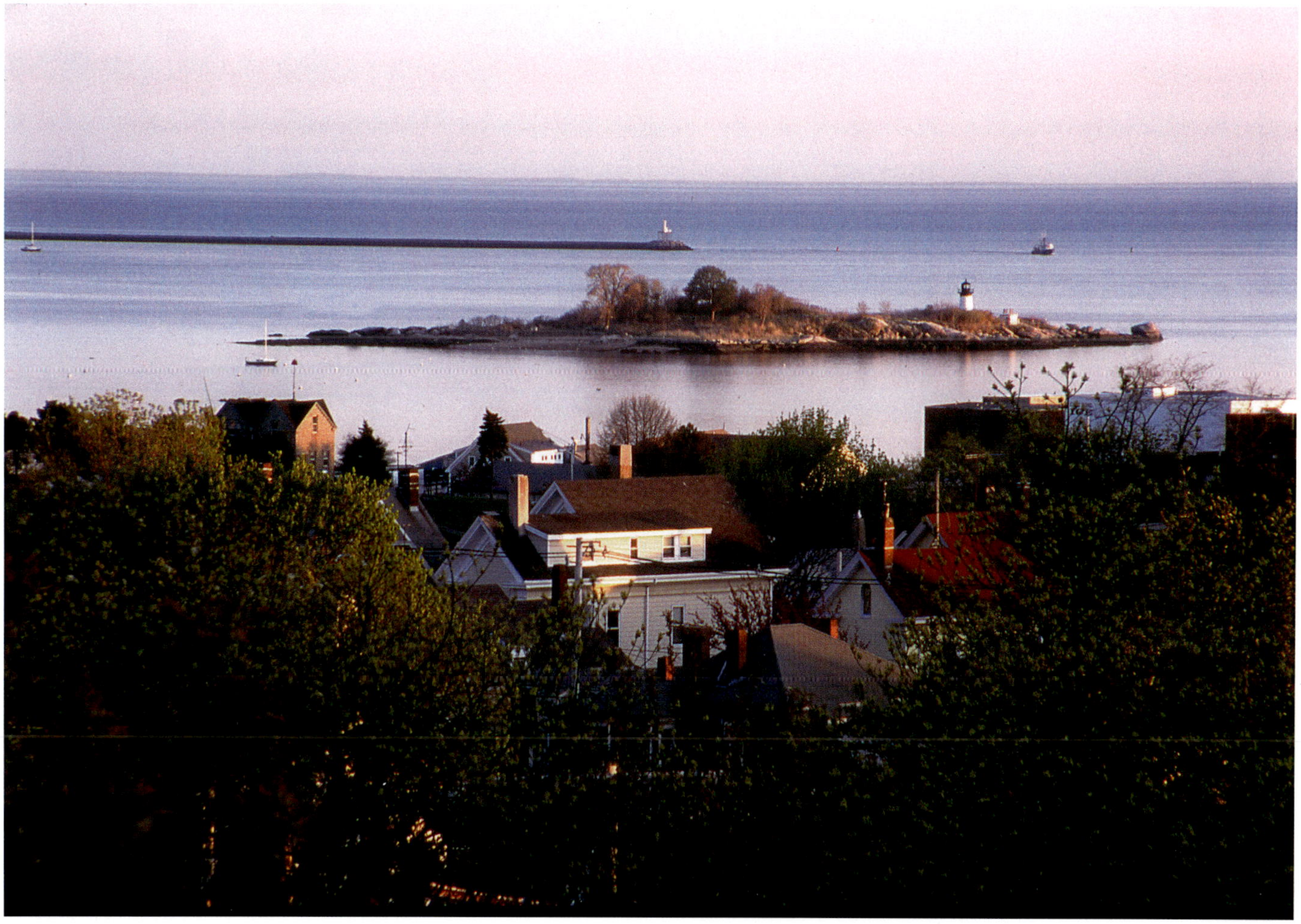

Fisherman's Memorial on Stacy Boulevard

Standing at the wheel, the Fisherman looks out over the sea as he has since 1923. He impressed me even when I was a kid in the '30s. I would note his verdigris strength as I read and reread the inscription set in the base of the monument: "They that go down to the sea in ships." I spent a lot of time on the boulevard hanging around or roller skating on the uneven sections of concrete with my friend Carolyn. I was also among the Girl Scouts and Boy Scouts who, accompanied by the Gloucester High School ROTC band, paraded to the monument for the annual memorial service for the fishermen, held in August. I can see the wreaths thrown from the bridge into the swirling waters of the outgoing tide. So many Gloucester families, including mine, have lost someone to the sea.

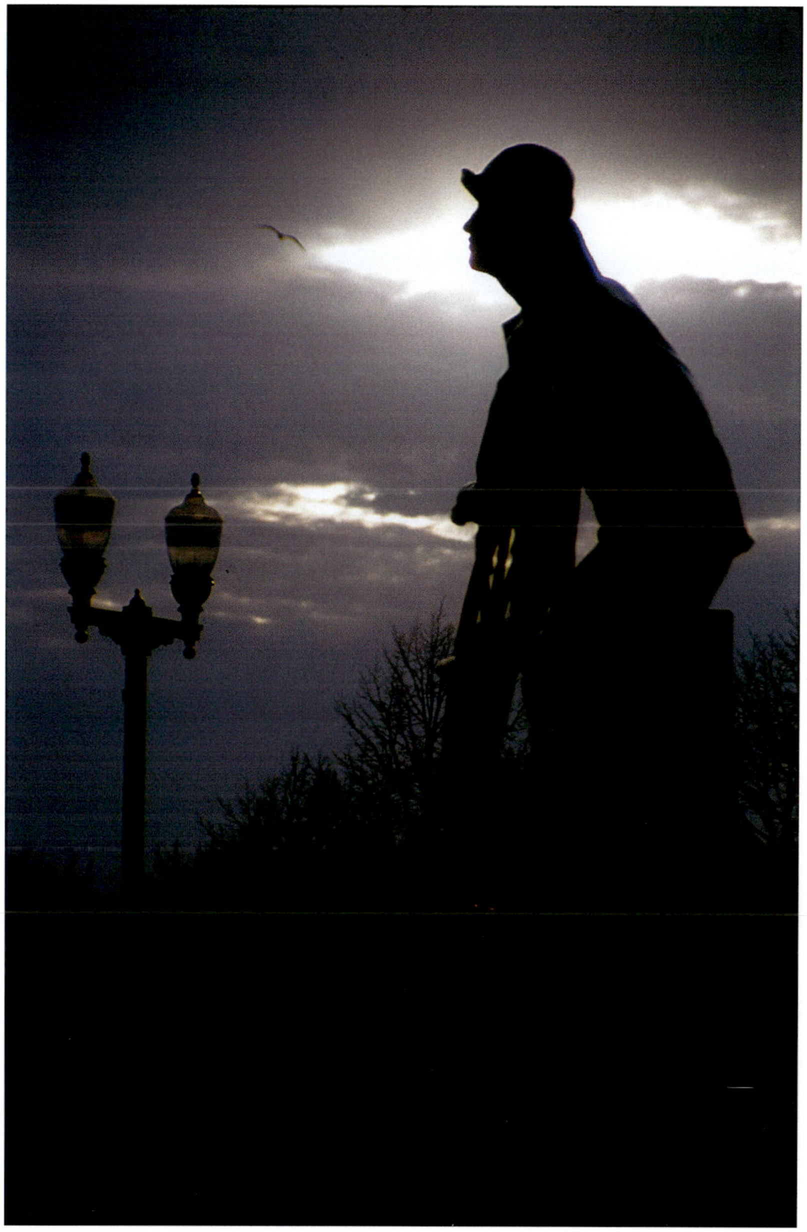

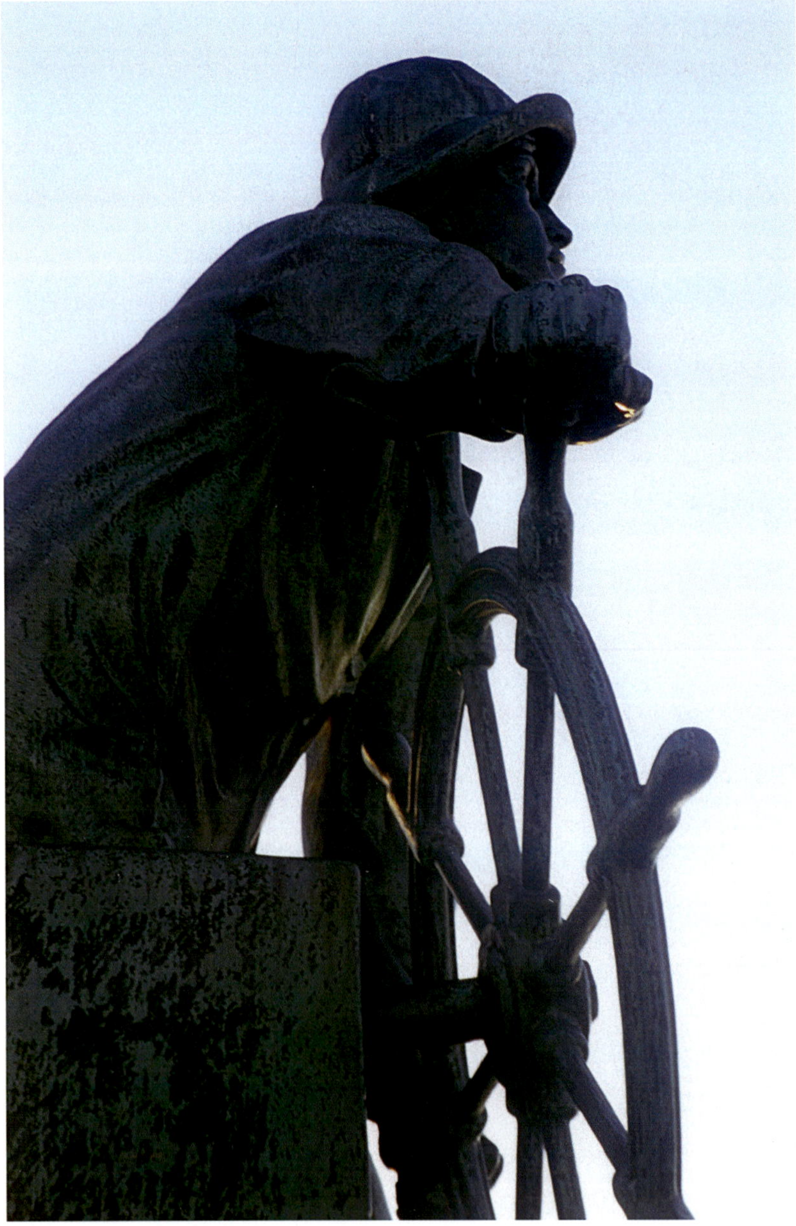

Fisherman's Memorial

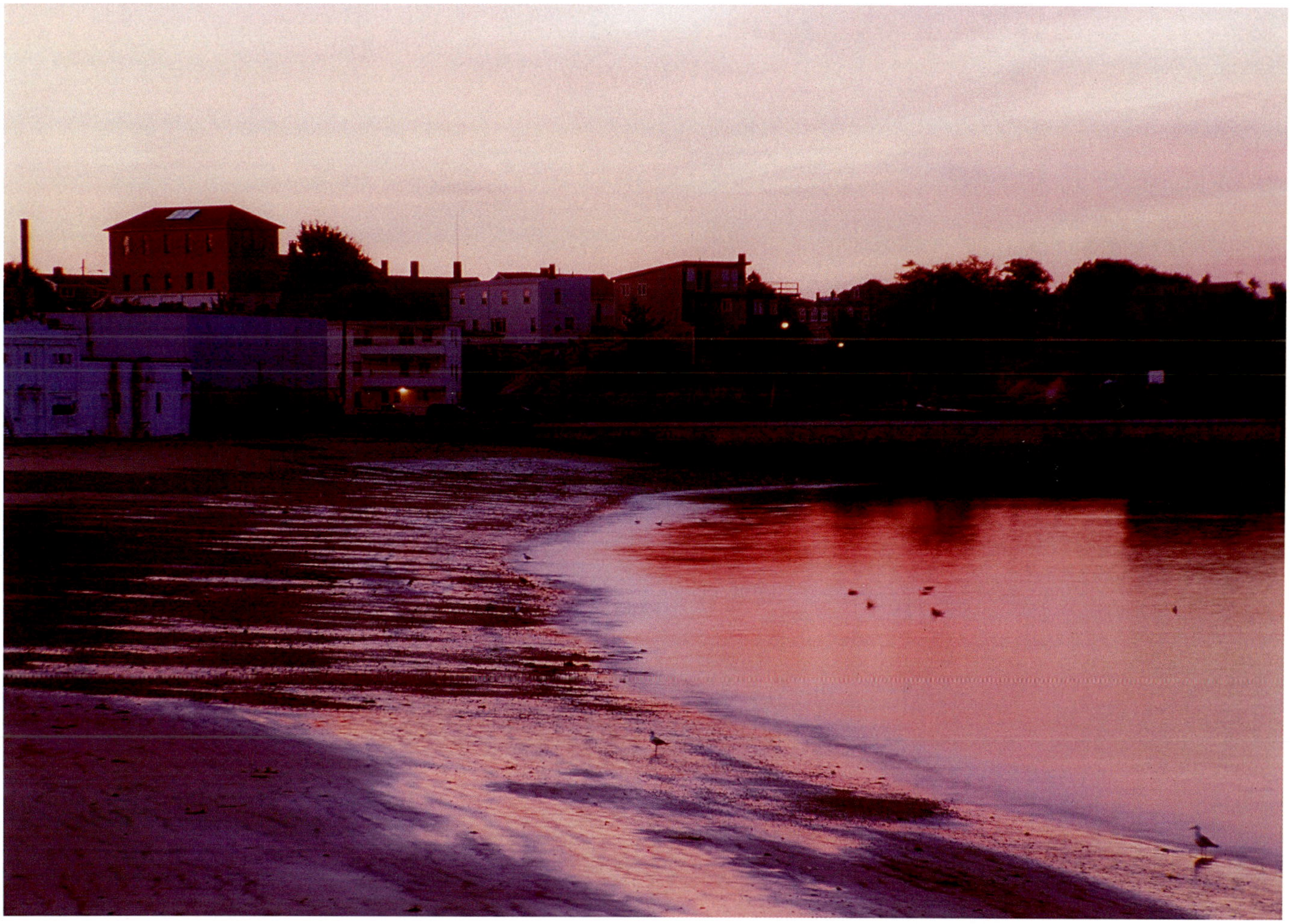

The Fort and Pavilion Beach at Dawn

The Rest House at Stage Fort Park

A summer day at Stage Fort Park always included a couple of visits to the Welcoming Center, which we knew then as the Rest House. On the main floor were a lounge and a concession area where we often stopped on our way home for a Popsicle.

One day in the summer of 1942 stands out in my mind. After my friend Nancy and I had arrived at Cressey's Beach, below the Rest House, we stopped briefly to talk with my older brother, Johnnie, who was the lifeguard. When Nancy suggested that we swim out to the raft, I thought, why not? I was sure I could do it. Part way there, though, with Nancy swimming easily ahead of me in the choppy water, I felt tired. And scared! Could I make it? If I went under, would Johnnie be able to swim out in time to rescue me? I paddled anxiously. Finally, the tips of my fingers touched the rough, wooden edge of the raft. I'd made it! I was safe! The swim back to shore later was no problem. The water was more calm. I wasn't scared.

After soaking up some sun, we trudged up the grassy incline to the Rest House for a Popsicle. I asked for orange. That day I wanted a powerful color and a strong flavor. I needed to be invigorated and revitalized!

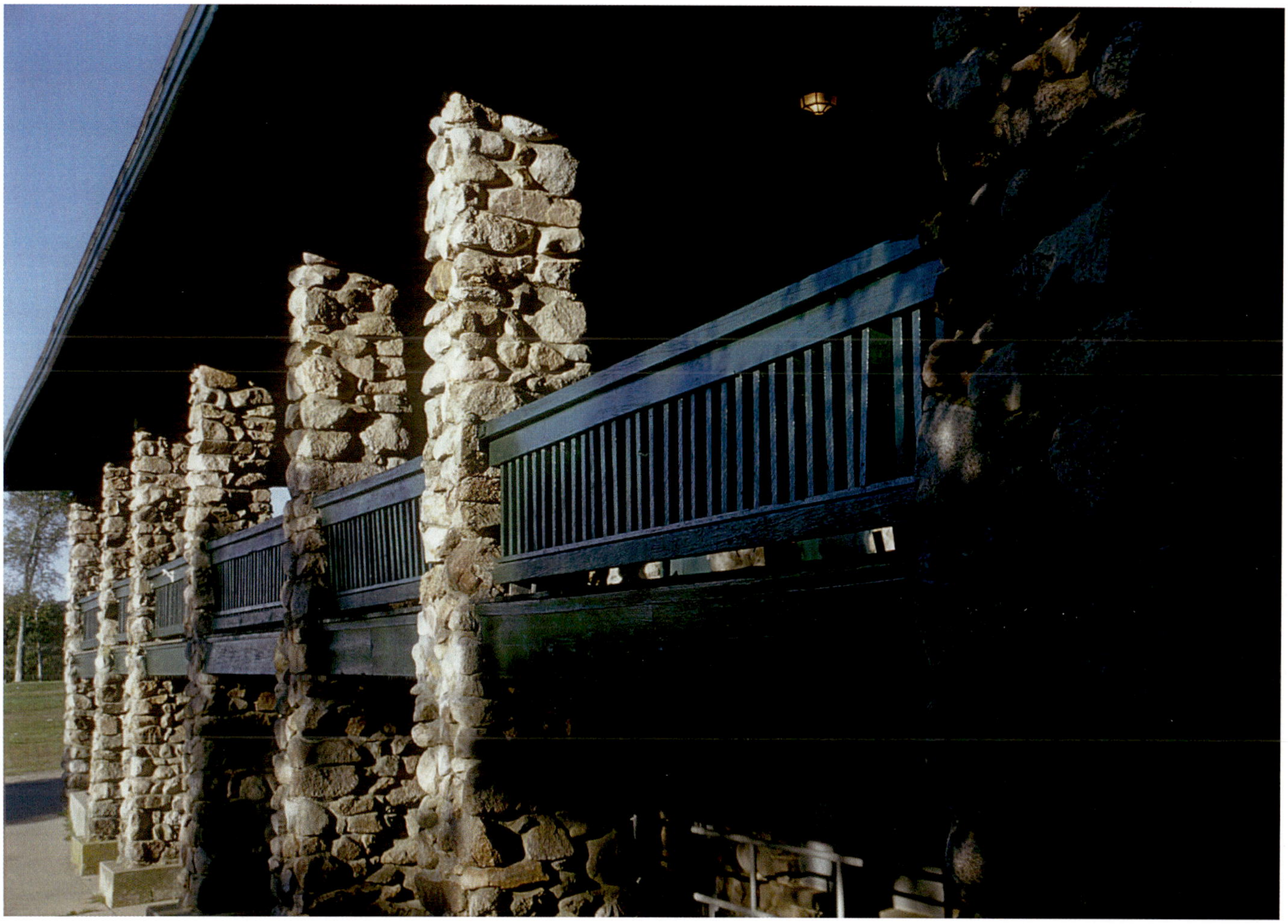

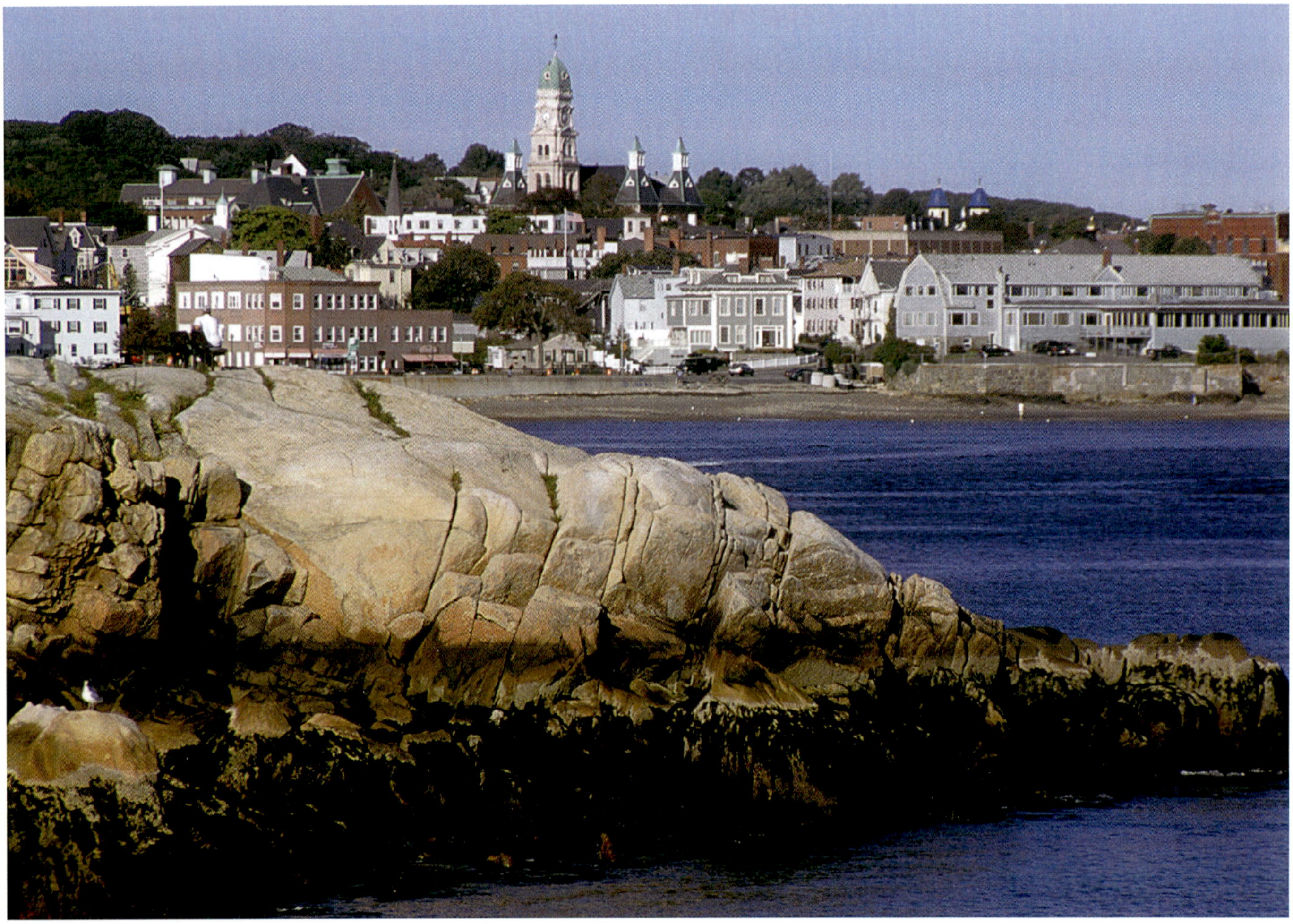

Half Moon Beach at Stage Fort Park

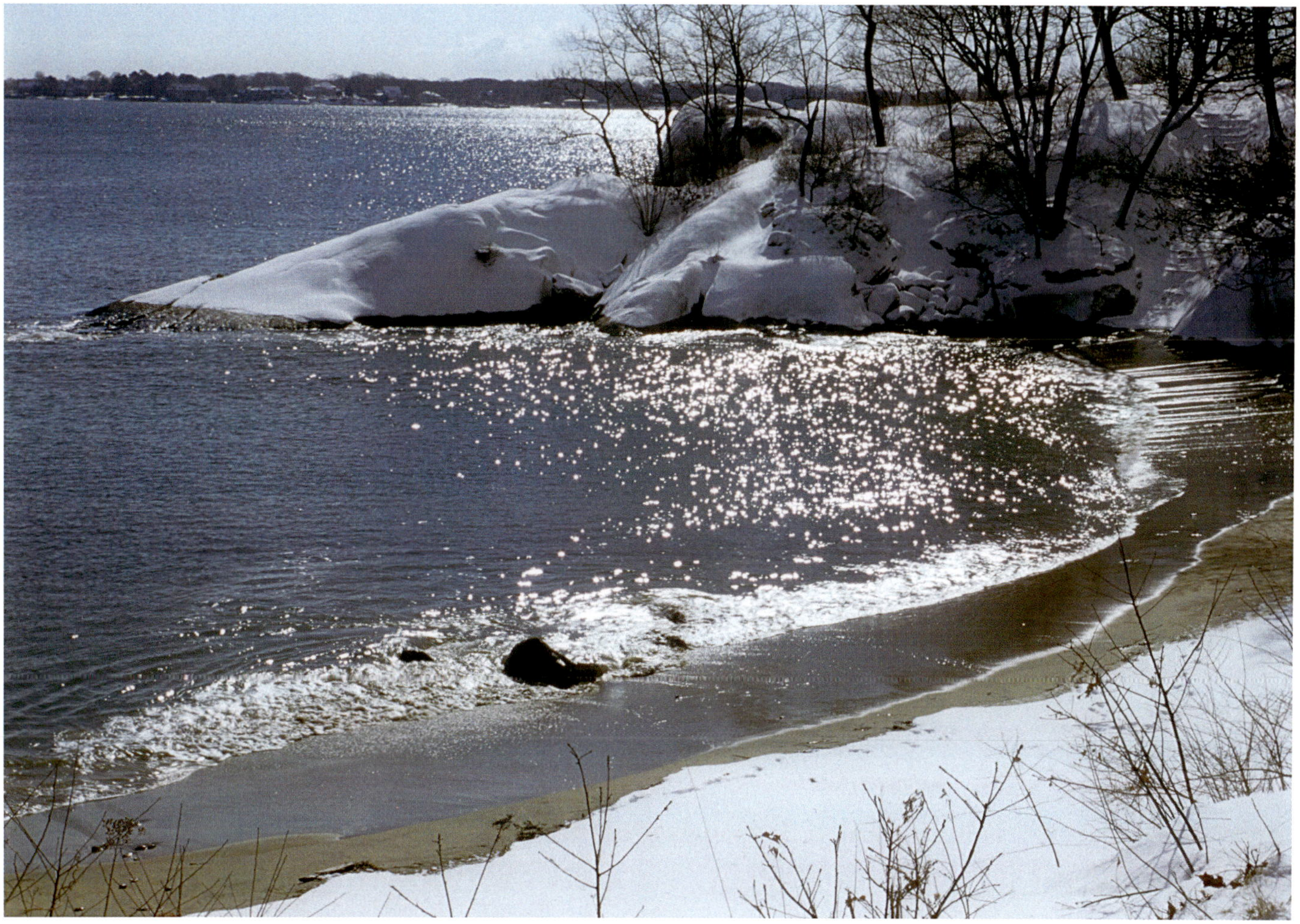

Half Moon Beach in Winter

Central Grammar, Room 38
1942–1943

Miss Anna S. Babson was my eighth grade Social Studies teacher. She'd been my father's teacher, too. Tall and elegant, her gray hair in a knot, she had a measured way of speaking and a warm smile. I noticed also that her wardrobe was quite limited. She had two identical dresses, one plum colored and one brown, very tailored. Sometimes, she wore a navy blue skirt and a long-sleeved white blouse trimmed with lace. That was all of her school clothing.

During Social Studies classes she stimulated my interest in travel by describing memorable sights around the world. One, I remember, was Cleopatra's Needle, an obelisk in London. Another was the Kattegat and the Skagarak, two bodies of water that converge on the northern coast of Denmark. In my travels, I've seen these sights and more. I wonder if Miss Babson ever did?

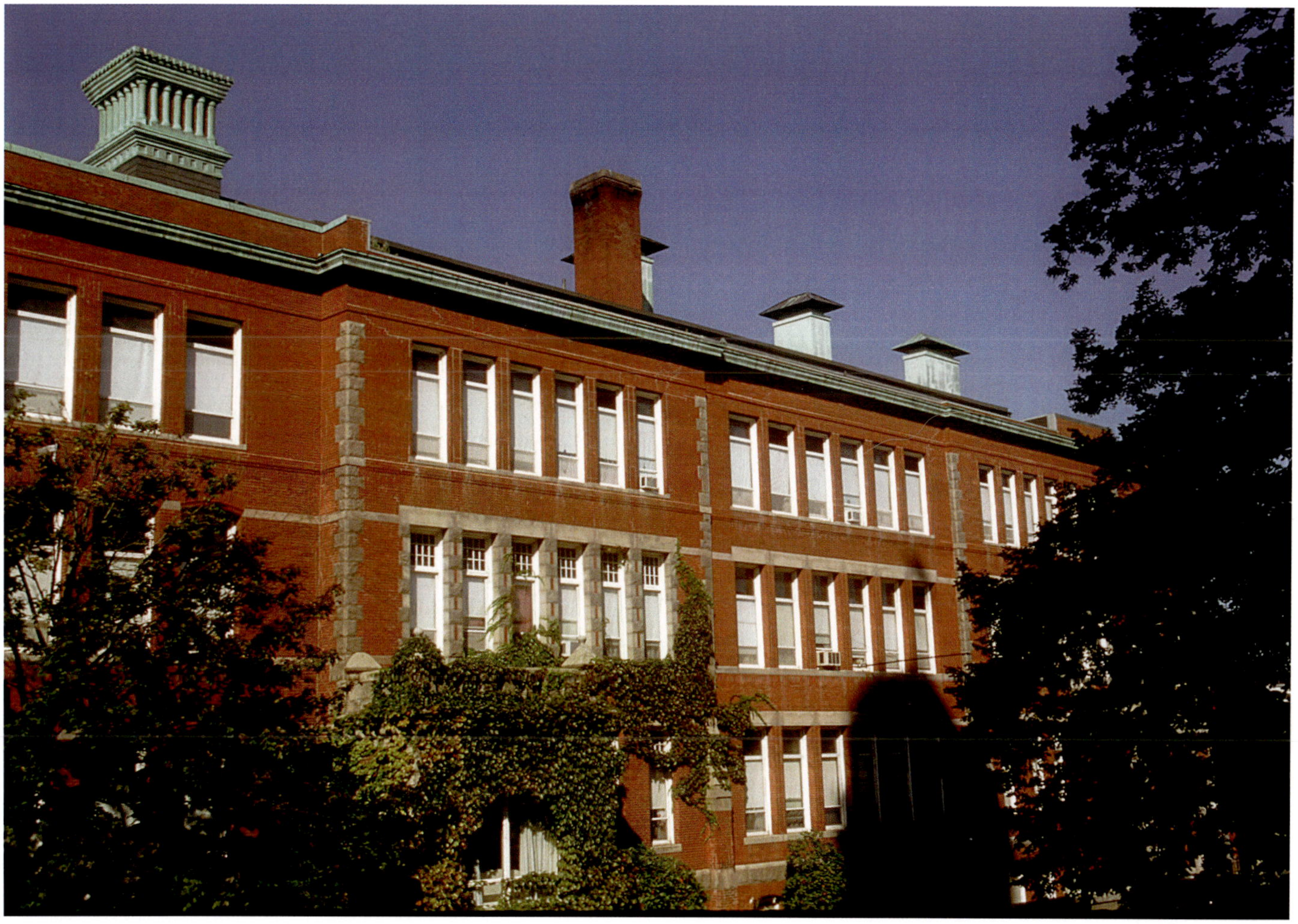

Sawyer Free Library, South Wing Stacks 1943–1947

Madame de Sevigne, I wrote as usual in the notebook we high school students had to sign before entering what is now the South Wing stacks. A student had misbehaved, irritating the librarians. (At that time before the addition was built, the South Wing stacks were the only stacks.)

When I visited these stacks a few years ago, reminiscing about the many hours I had spent reading there, all seemed the same, except for carpeting on the floor and on the metal stairs. I did observe that there was no notebook to sign. I've often wondered through the years—did the librarians laugh at my joke?

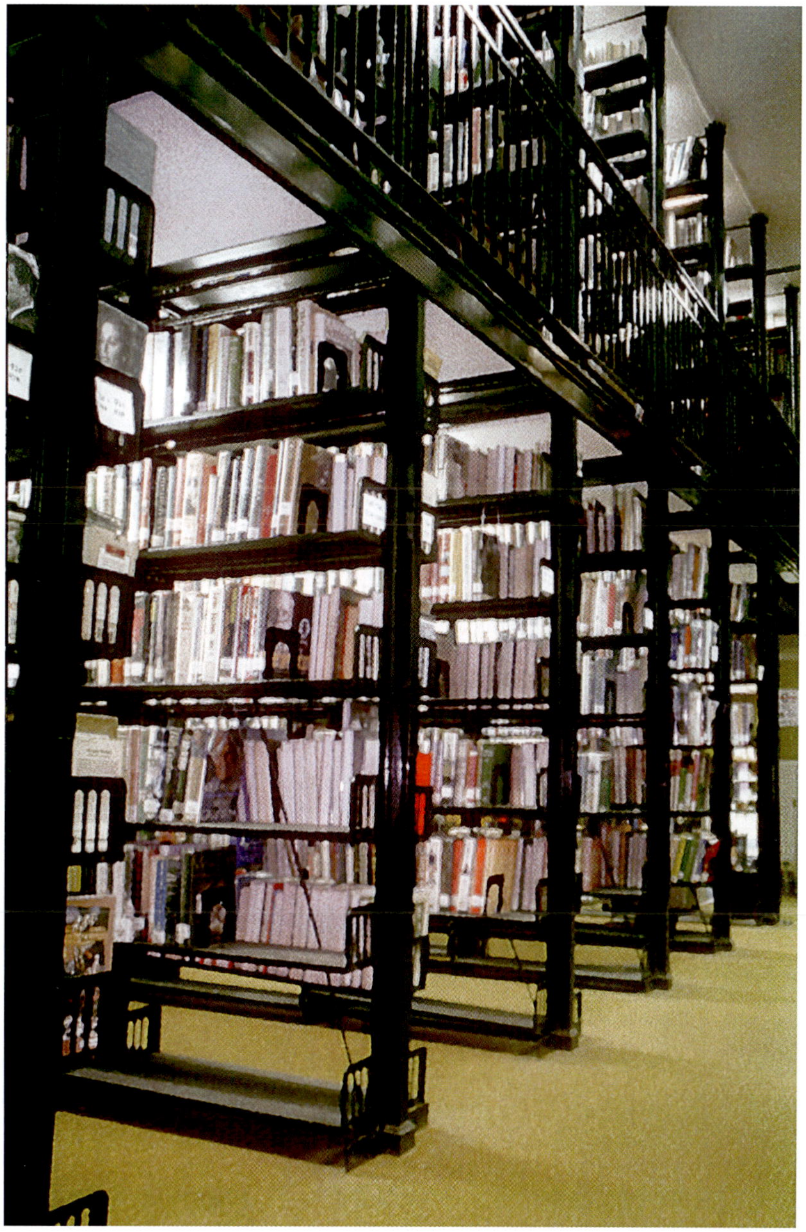

Administration Building–1944

Up the stairs I climbed to the second floor of the Gloucester School Administration building at 7 Beacon Street, now a private home. Joe Bentley, truant officer for the local school system and supervisor of work papers for kids under sixteen, was waiting for me. A friend of my family, he welcomed me and helped me fill out my papers.

He asked me if I had a job. I certainly did! (This was wartime. Companies were short staffed and willing to hire people as young as I was—fifteen.) I was going to be candling red fish for Progressive Fish Company on Commercial Street.

I told Joe that the job was simple. I'd move the fillets quickly over a lighted glass area and cut out any sores or "buttons" on the fish. Little did I realize how boring this would be. Over and over again, all day long, I would do this job. But the pay was good and would help pay for my college education.

Thank you Joe Bentley for your encouragement and for starting me on my way!

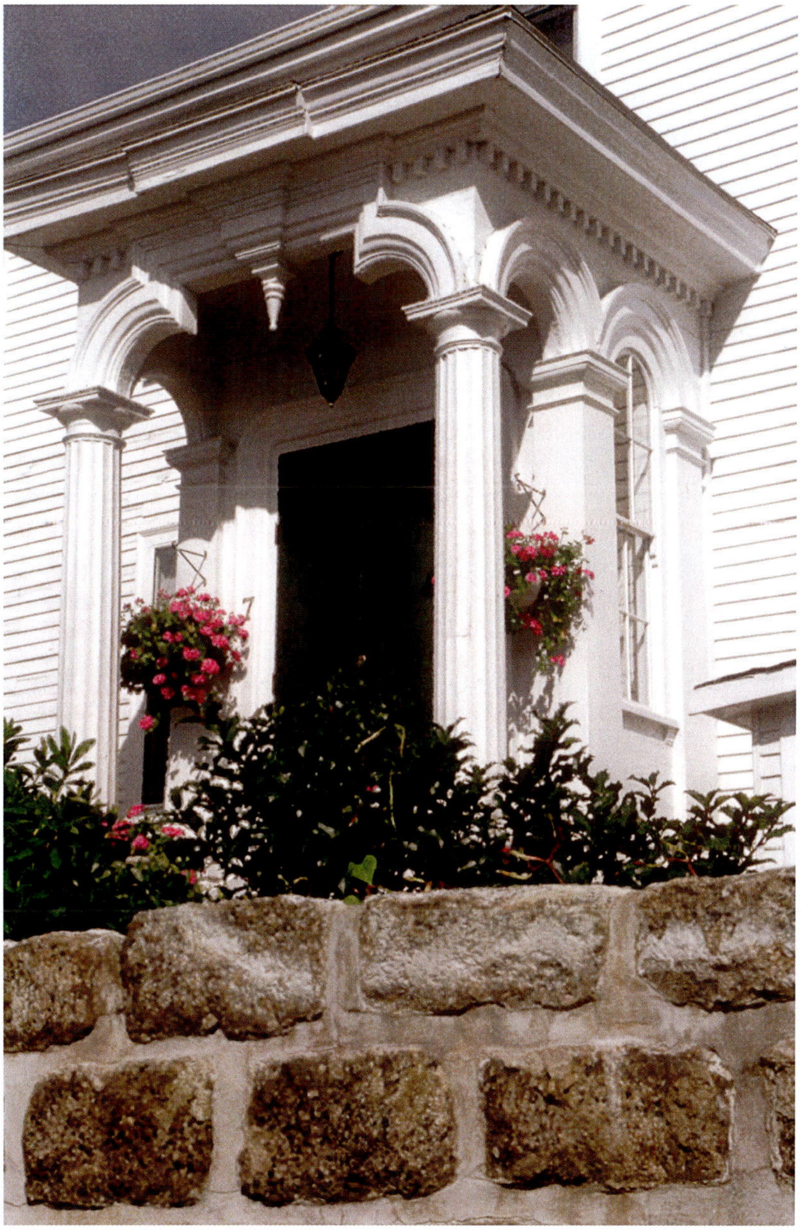

The Boulevard at Dawn–1946

It was just getting light on an early spring morning in 1946 when my mother's dog, Sally, and I hustled across the boulevard. Sally, a high-strung Dalmation with a tail like a whip, tugged on her leash, hurrying me along. There were no other dogs to be seen or people, either. Not that day or any other day, then. An occasional car or truck. Otherwise, it was just Sally and me. (I remember thinking how safe I felt with her. She was young and strong and would take care of me, I knew.) Back and forth on the boulevard we raced, then up Centennial Avenue to our home on Beacon Street for breakfast. Then it was Gloucester High School for me and a nap for Sally. What a great way to start the day!

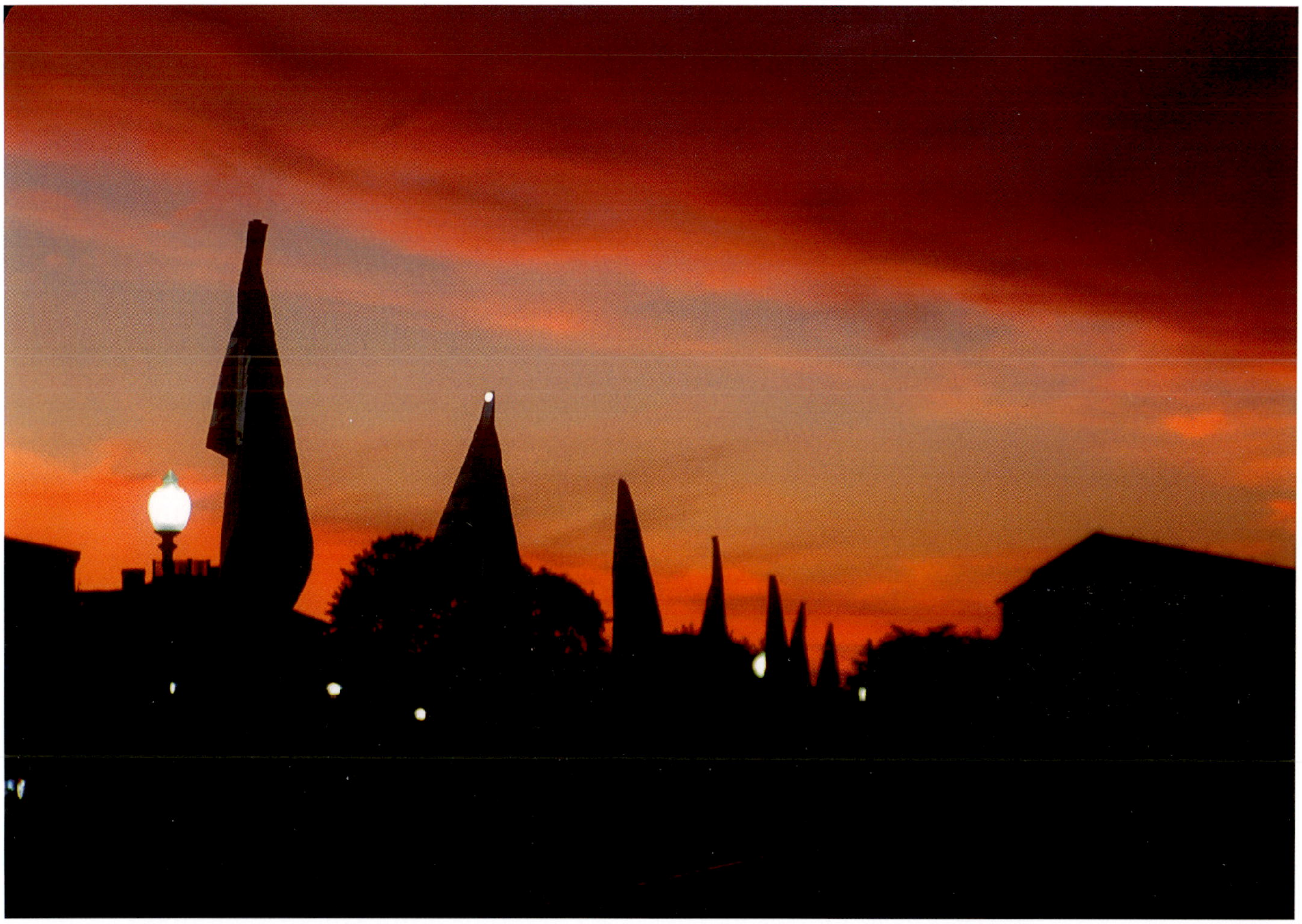

Winter on Rocky Neck–February 1946

I should have been home studying for the weekly French test given by "Henry," my French teacher at Gloucester High School, but instead I was hanging around with my friends on a late winter Sunday afternoon. We'd taken the bus from downtown Gloucester and met Julia, a classmate, who lived over here.

What I remember so well, as we walked aimlessly here and there in the art colony, was the lifeless off-season feeling of the area. All the shops, galleries and restaurants were closed tightly against winter. While most of the businesses in Gloucester were also closed today since it was Sunday, I felt the dullness, the silence and loneliness more here. Downtown Gloucester would come alive on Monday morning, but the businesses on Rocky Neck would remain silent.

Winter was too long, I thought. I was tired of the lack of activity; I was tired of the dirty snow. Then I glanced down at the water in Smith Cove. The ice was breaking up around the Studio Restaurant piers. Spring would come soon.

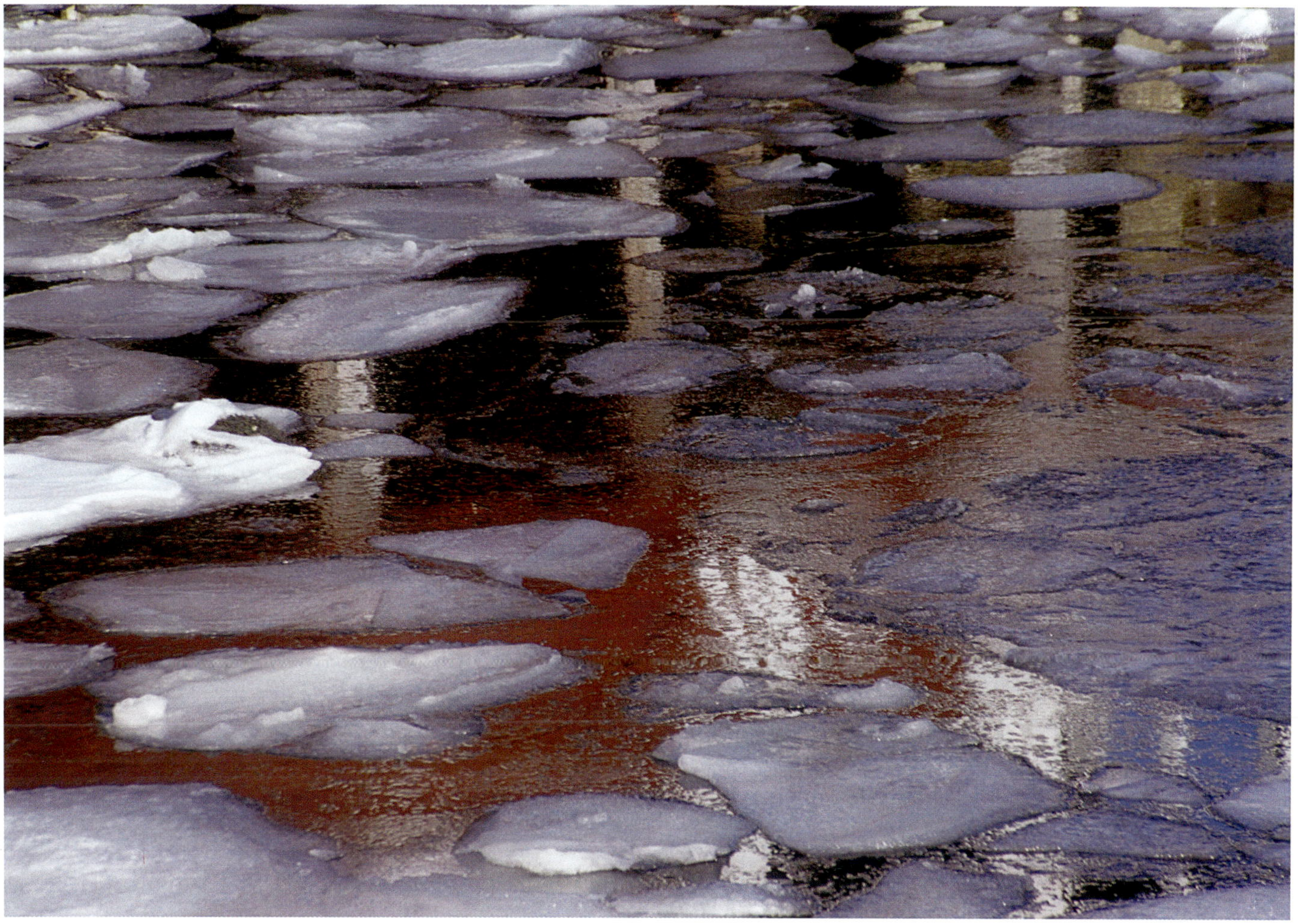

W. G. Brown & Co. Pleasant Street Building 1945–1947

I was #8 on the dial of the time clock we employees punched. I made $14.64 a week working from 8:45AM to 5:30PM most days with Wednesday afternoon off and from 11:00AM to 9:00PM on Saturday.

I started in Notions, then located in the center aisle on the first floor of the Main Street building. Bit by bit, I learned about buttons, thread and all kinds of sewing incidentals. Later, I was transferred to many different departments, but I liked being in the center of the store best, where I could see everyone coming and going, and walking up and down the stairs to the second floor of the Main Street building or to the adjoining Pleasant Street building. As the public address system would sound—a musical bong—a different number of times for each of the four Brown executives, I'd count to see who was being summoned. Occasionally, I'd look up at the large clock suspended from the ceiling to see how much more time until closing or how soon on a Saturday I could have my supper. I can almost smell the Salisbury steak that John, the chef, regularly prepared at the lunch counter on the far wall of the store. I am ever grateful for my experiences working for the W. G. Brown Company in Gloucester. I learned so much about merchandise and people.

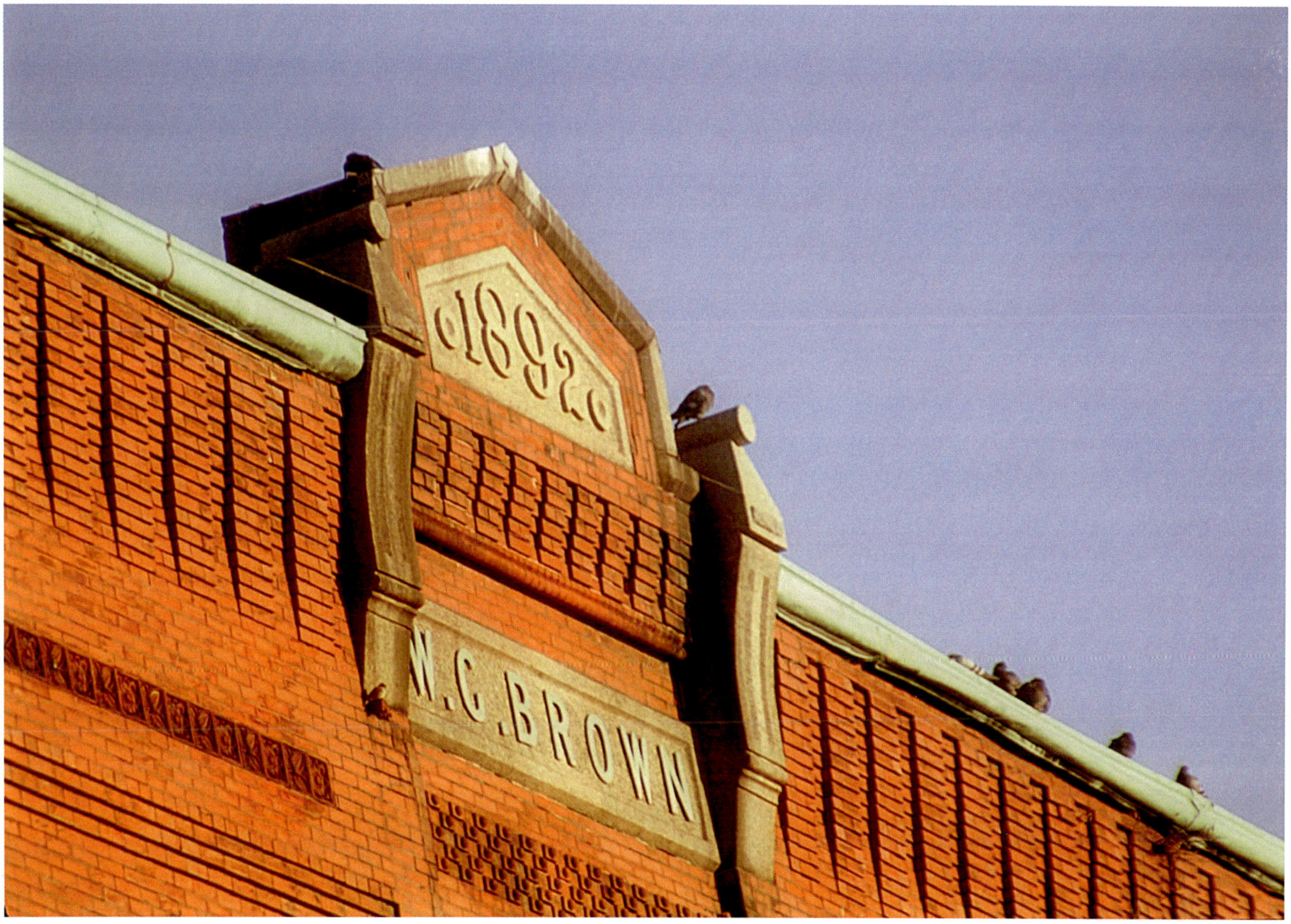
1892
W.C. BROWN

Nick's Pool Parlor

The sound of pool balls whacking one another, the acrid smell of cigarette smoke, cat calls and leering looks! What high school girls of the 1940s will forget what it was like to have to walk by Nick's Pool Parlor at 124 Main Street (now an antique shop) in order to go to Towle's, where we girls would gab in a booth while we enjoyed an ice cream soda? Many times I crossed the street so I wouldn't have to walk by those obnoxious boys!

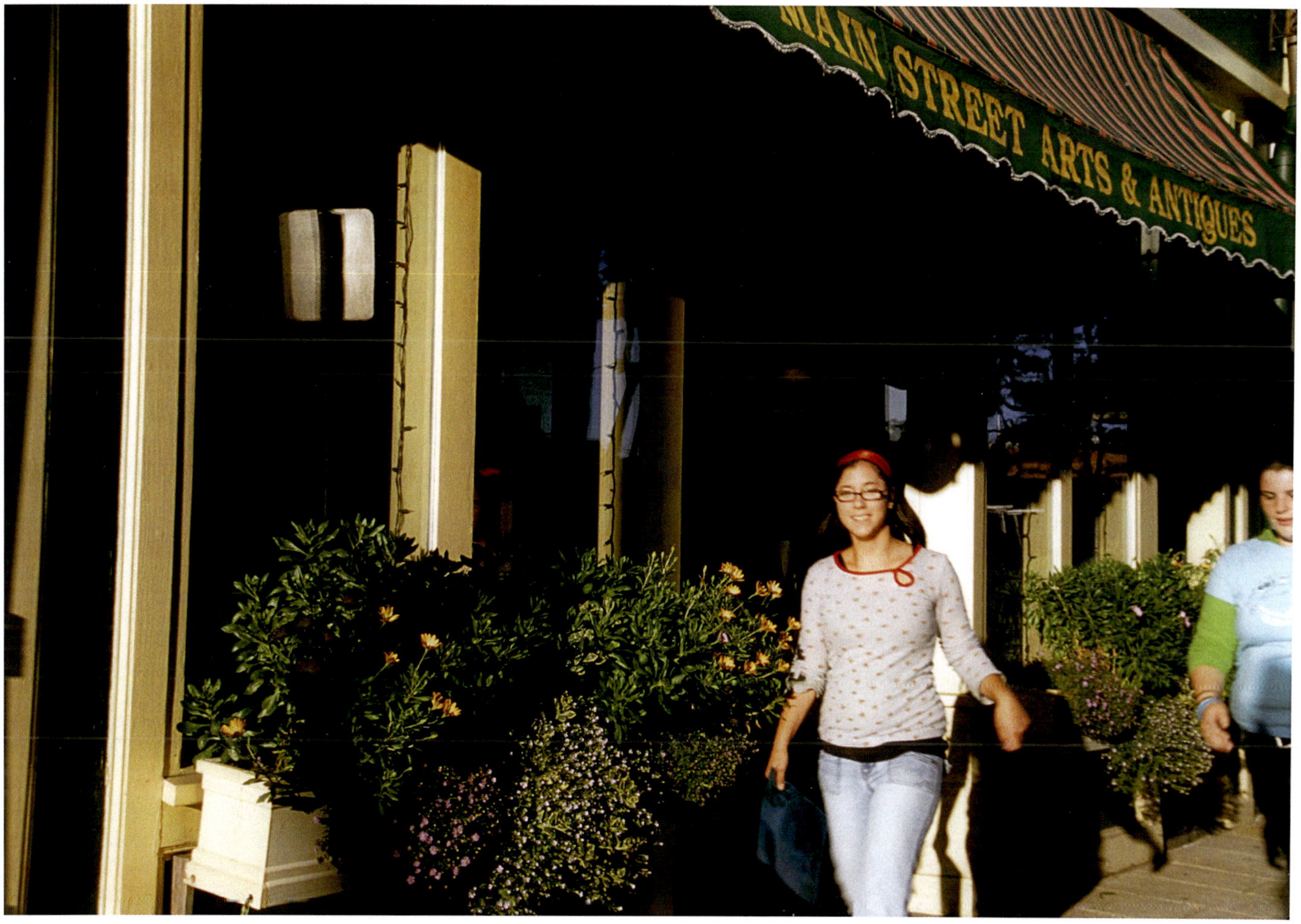
MAIN STREET ARTS & ANTIQUES

Wonson's Cove–February 1, 1947

It was a bitter-cold winter night. Stepping off the East Gloucester bus at Eastern Point Boulevard, my friends Harriet and Joey and I crunched our way through the icy snow past Wonson's Cove. Warmly dressed in our winter gear including the latest fashion—knee-high rubber boots—we didn't mind the cold. We were high school seniors and young! Up the hill we climbed and after a short walk we had arrived at Niles Beach. Niles Beach? Yes, we'd come to celebrate my eighteenth birthday. In a small bag I carried three pieces of my birthday cake—cake my mother had baked for me the day before on my birthday. As we huddled together on the beach they sang *Happy Birthday* to me. How lucky I was to have such good friends willing to accept my zany invitation. Happy Birthday, indeed.

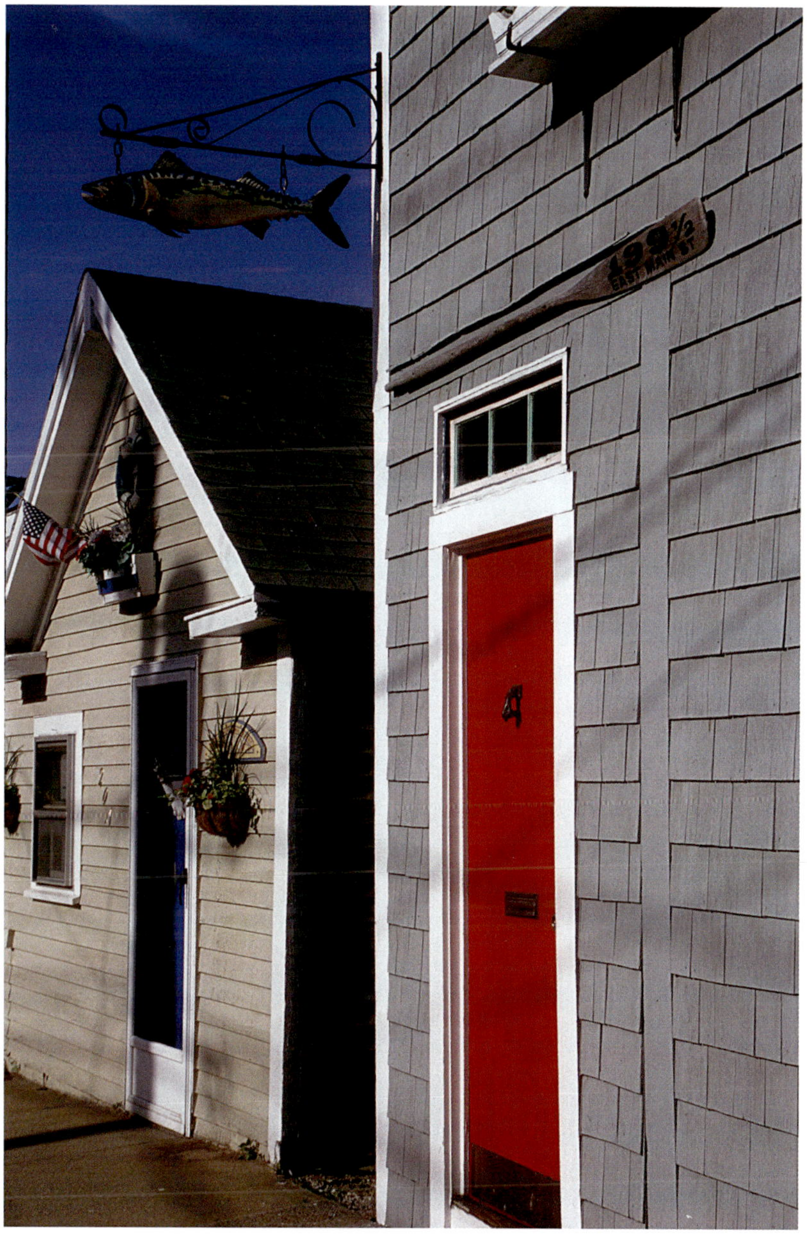

Typical Gloucester Homes near the Bowling Alleys

Rocky Neck in the Summer–1950

Stylish galleries, enticing restaurants, tourists and flowers everywhere they could grow! In summer, Rocky Neck had a vibrant quality. It was so different from winter with its stark, quiet beauty.

One of my fondest memories of Rocky Neck in the summer, during my college years, is the evening my mother and I took the bus from town to see the Little Theater's production of Thornton Wilder's play, *Our Town*. (The theater, long gone, was located next to the Marine Railway.) We smiled and wept our way through the performance.

Rereading the play recently brought back memories of that long ago summer evening.

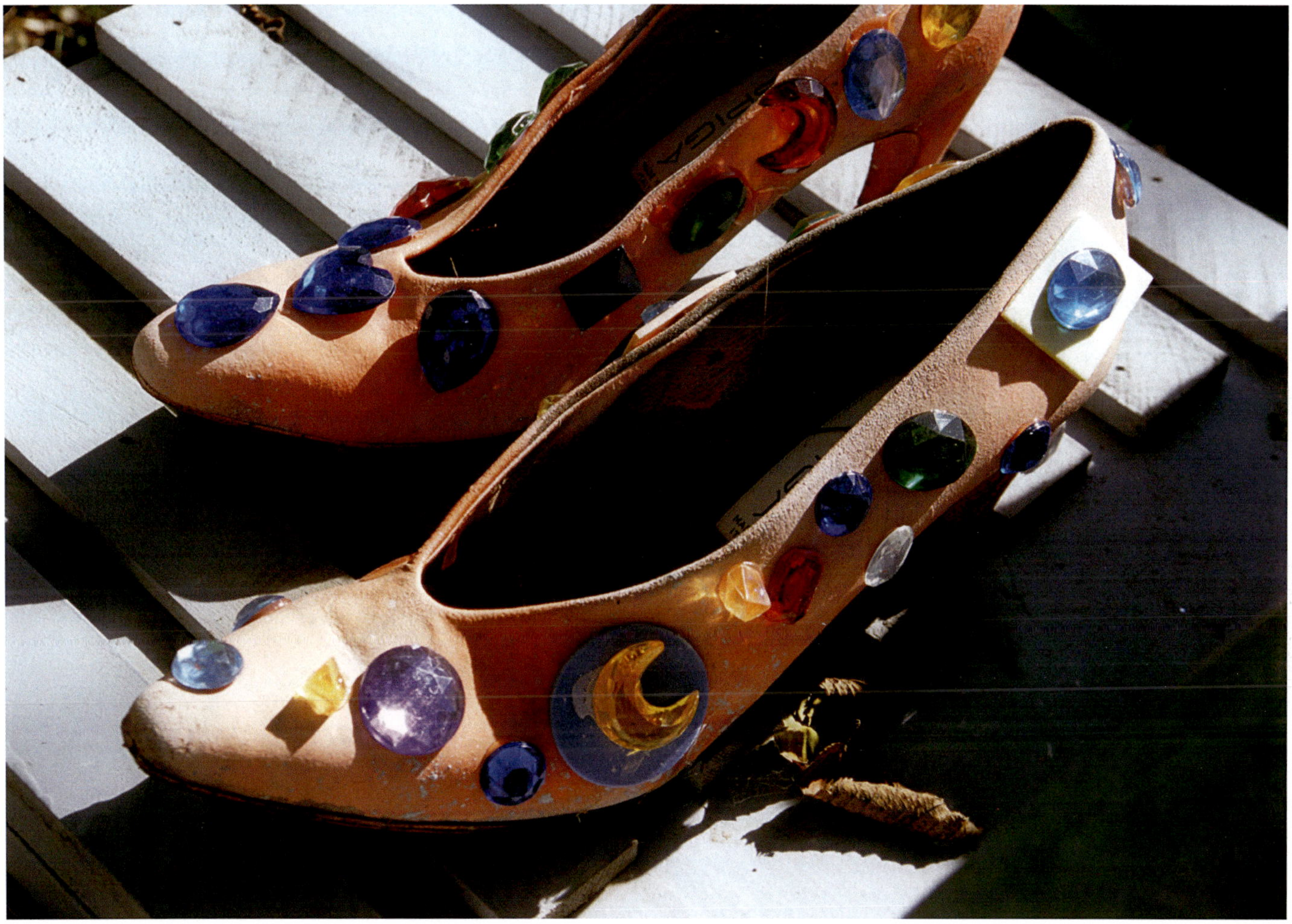

Wonson's Paint Factory–1950

Picture a warm, sunny summer day back in 1950. My boyfriend, Dave, (soon to be my husband), his father and I have rented a boat from Jerry Hill at Rocky Neck. Dave rowed the boat close to the paint factory where we three fished for flounder and pollock. We caught some, too! But I realized that I'd rather study the reflections of the paint factory than touch those slimy sea worms!

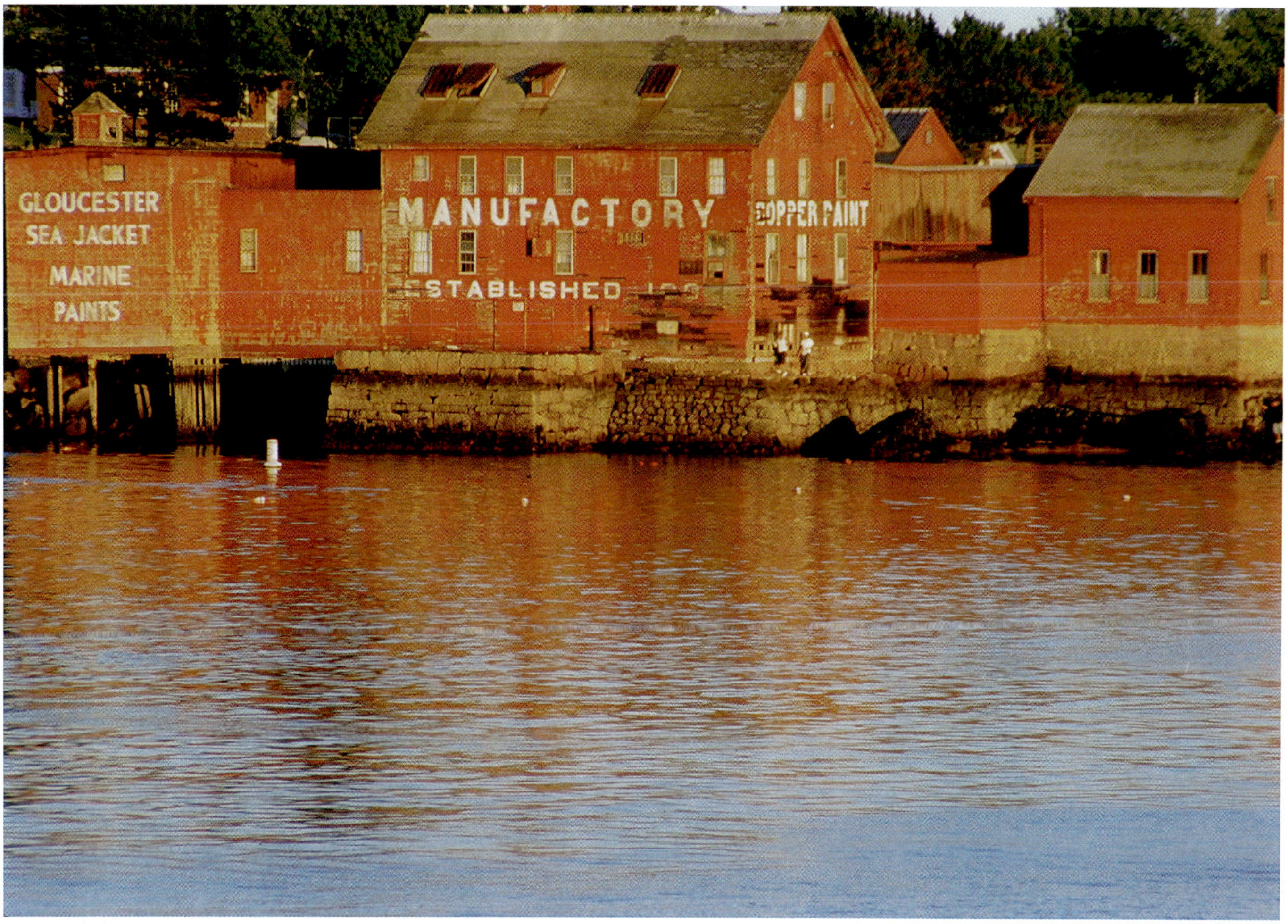
GLOUCESTER
SEA JACKET
MARINE
PAINTS
MANUFACTORY
COPPER PAINT
ESTABLISHED

Empire Fish Company—1951
The Last Place Where I Packed Fish

Teddy, the boss, barks: "You, you and you—panning whiting in the big shed."

Me: "Oh, no, not that sloppy job again! Head, tail, head, tail, head, tail—fast, fast, fast! Even with the big rubber apron, I'll be soaked!"

Later:

Me: "I was right. I am soaked. Even my red oxfords are soaked."

"Buzzzzzz!" The harsh but welcome break-time buzzer sounds.

Me: "Mug-up—thank heaven!"

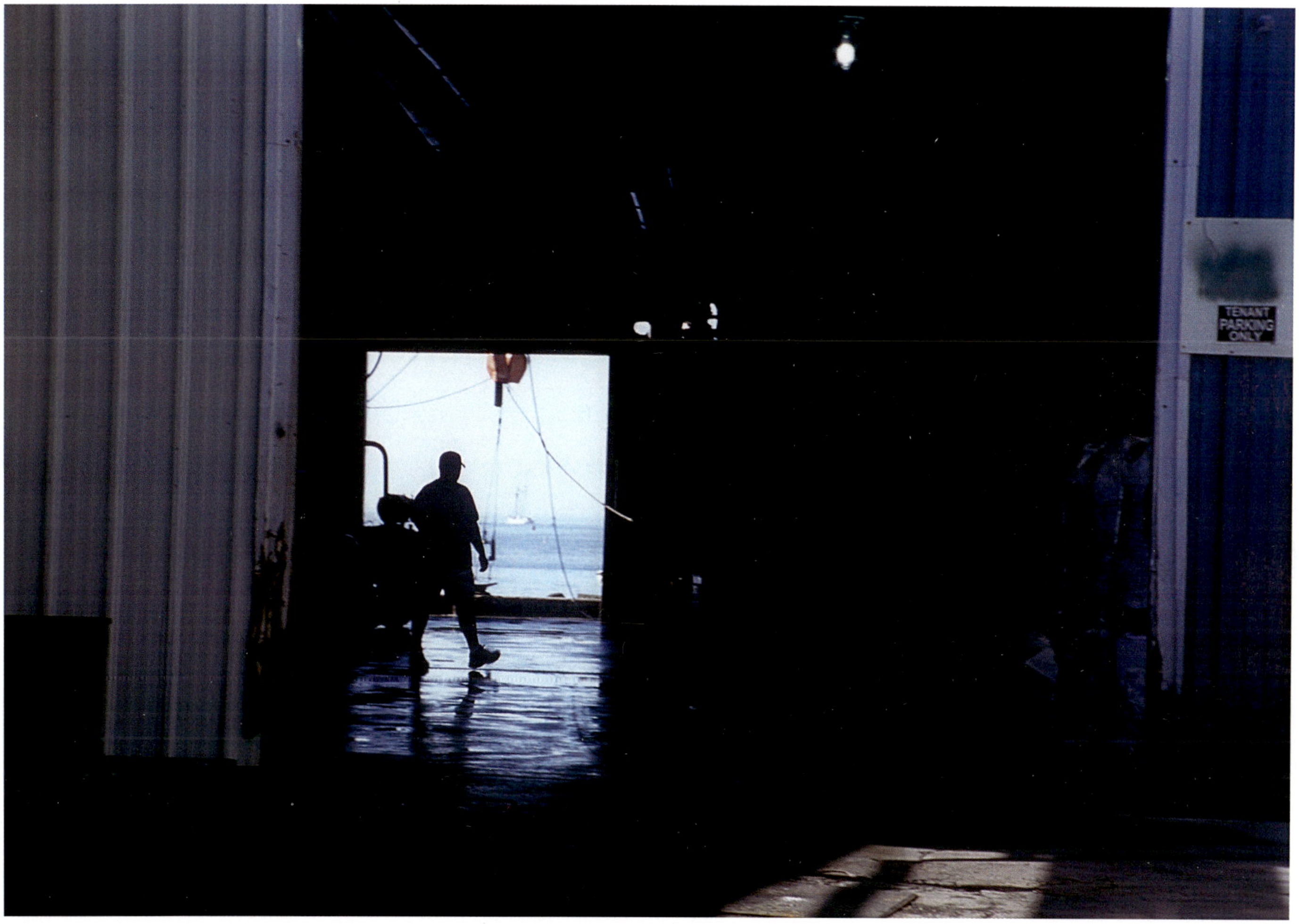
TENANT
PARKING
ONLY

Piers on Rogers Street

During my summers as a fish worker, I'd eat lunch with my sister, Margie, at the end of one of the piers. We'd laugh and joke as we ate our lunch.

I don't remember that there were any swans here, then. Now they're here and there in the harbor. This one was very obliging. While I focused on the pilings with my camera, completely ignoring a nearby swan, I was amused when he swam into my range. He seemed to be posing for me. He swam this way and that way. Then he circled the pilings several times, allowing me to get some good images. Talk about the luck of the Irish!

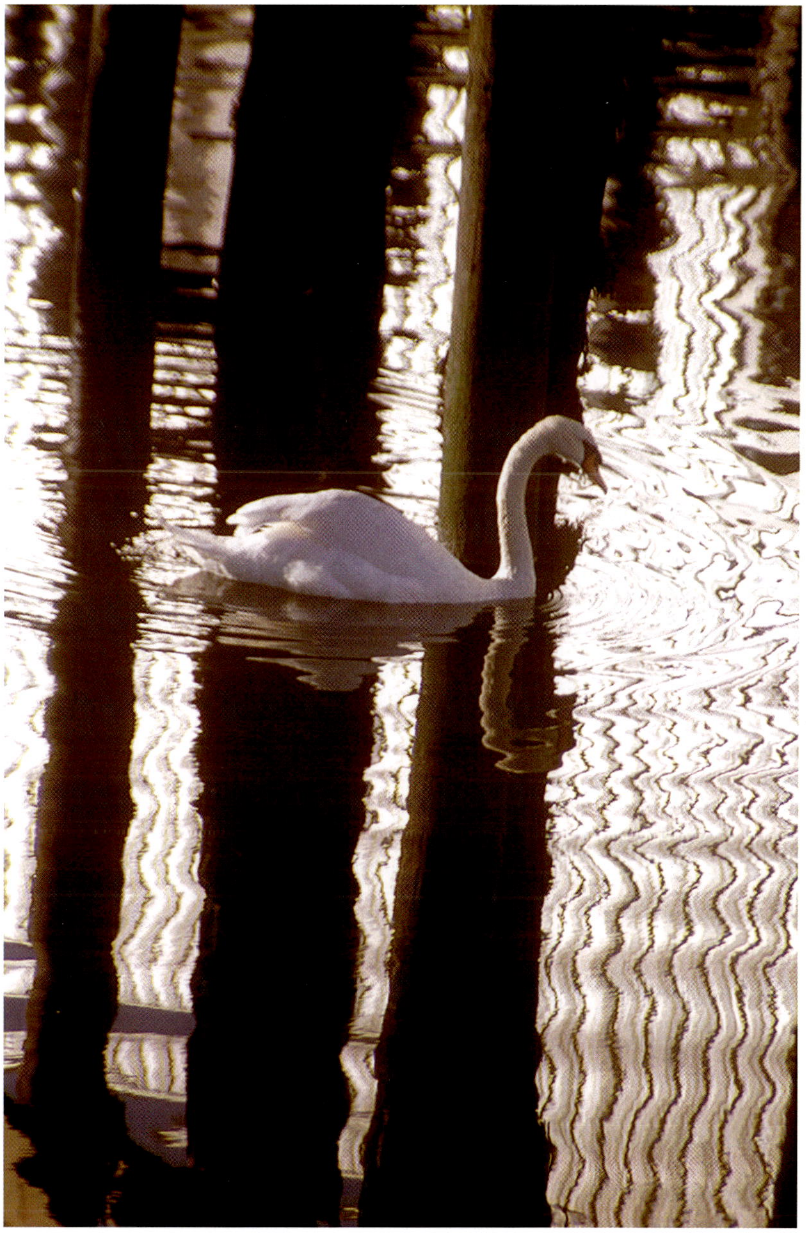

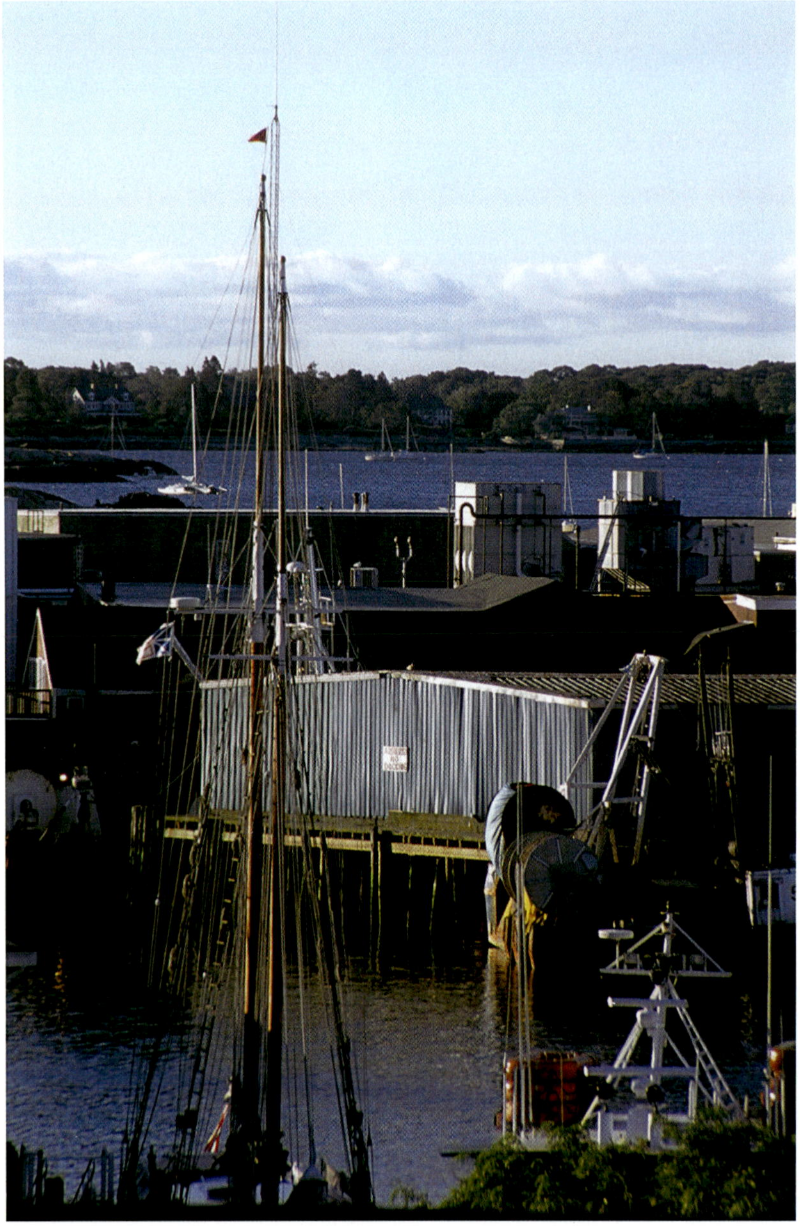

Waterfront View from the Cape Ann Savings Bank

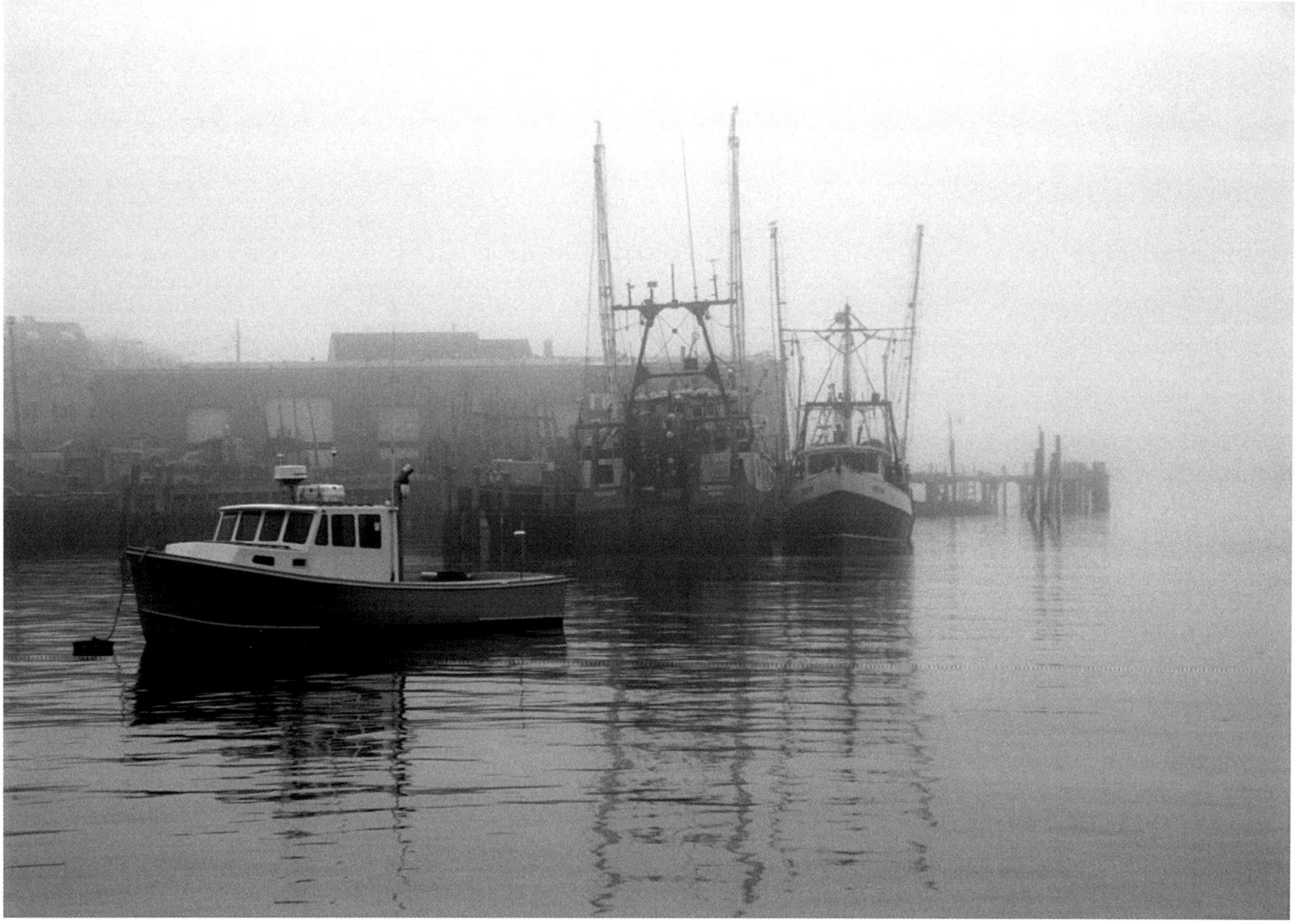

Foggy Waterfront

Town Landing during Fiesta Week

When I was growing up, the harbor was full of boats. The wharves were so busy! When the mackerel was in, I'd work from seven in the morning until nine at night in Gorton's cannery. Now it's very quiet down here. The cannery is gone. Some buildings are boarded up. There is a big empty space on the waterfront where several fish companies were located.

Gloucester is waiting…

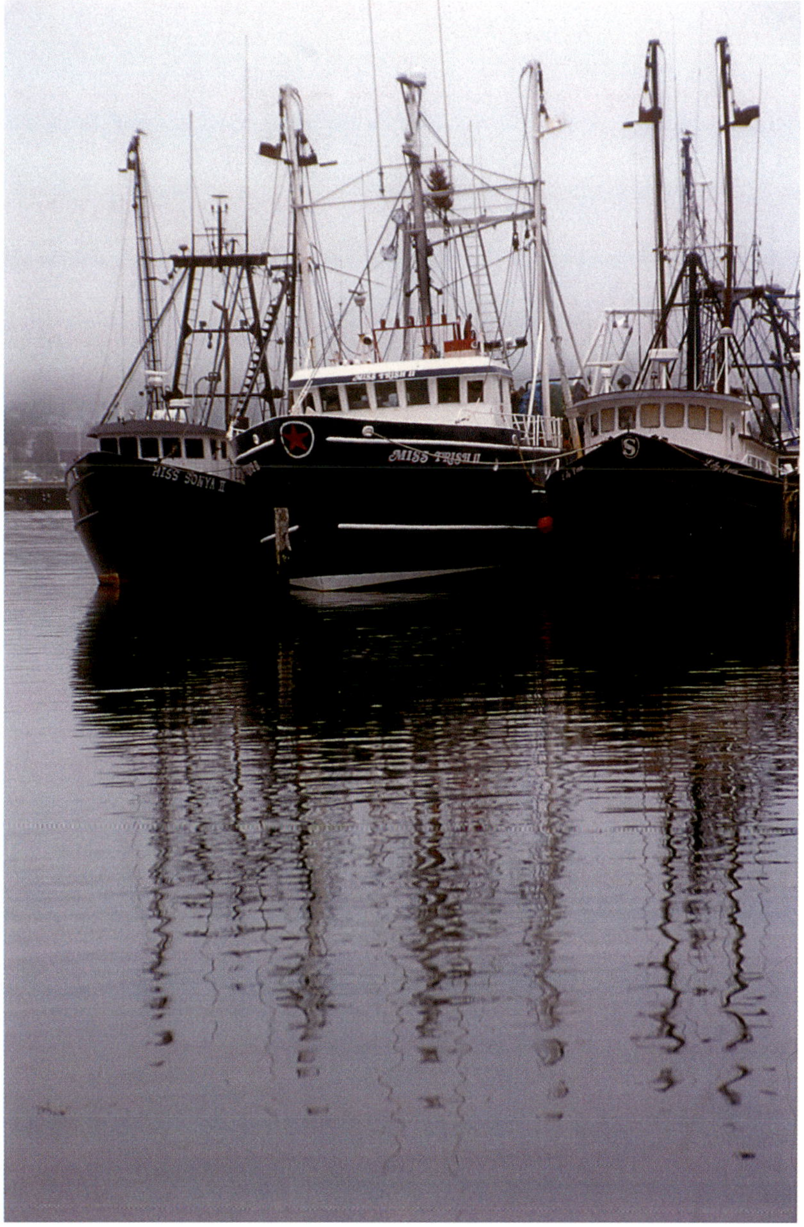
MISS SONYA II
MISS TRISH II

Lower Washington Street

Below my Dad's store, located on the corner of Washington and Prospect Streets, is what I call Lower Washington Street.

My friends and I walked down this way every week in our grade school years to Girl Scout meetings at the Community House.

We hung around here too, playing with kids in the neighborhood. Sometimes we'd visit the First National store to flirt with Pete, the young sandy-haired butcher!

Walking down this way now, I see things that you'll only see when you're on foot. A tiny garden, tucked between two houses, practically touching each other, caught my eye. There was a religious statue in the back of the garden. As I stood there, admiring the scene, the man of the house came out. "Which saint is this?" I asked. "It's St.Joseph," was his answer. Not knowing much about saints, I asked further, "What is he the patron saint of?" "He's the patron saint of carpenters," the man answered. "Jesus' father was a carpenter, you know." His answer was given in a kindly way with no looking down on my ignorance.

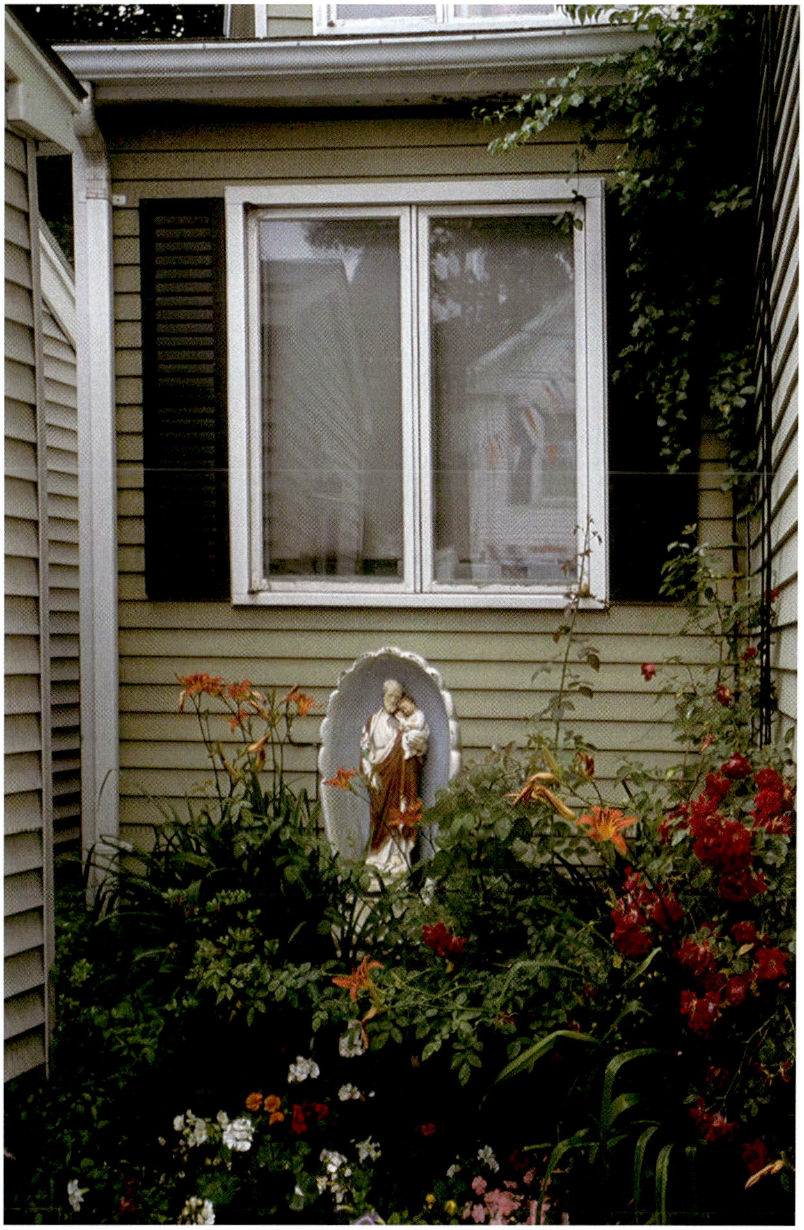

Mother of Grace Club
Lower Washington Street

The doors of the club building were usually shut securely, but on a warm September evening a couple of years ago they were wide open, giving a clear view of the interior. Women, mostly older ones, were seated facing the back of the building where the altar and the Blessed Virgin were located. They were praying intently, their voices lowered. Outside, the front of the building was decorated with silver metallic paper, almost covered with flowers. So beautiful! In the closed off street, musicians were playing Italian songs for a small audience sitting on folding chairs.

As I took in this scene I was thinking of the telephone calls the ladies regularly made to my Dad when he served as a city councilor from the 1940s through the 1960s. When they needed help they called him, knowing that they could count on him. "Mr. O'Connell, could you...?" Yes, he could. It was his pleasure to serve the people.

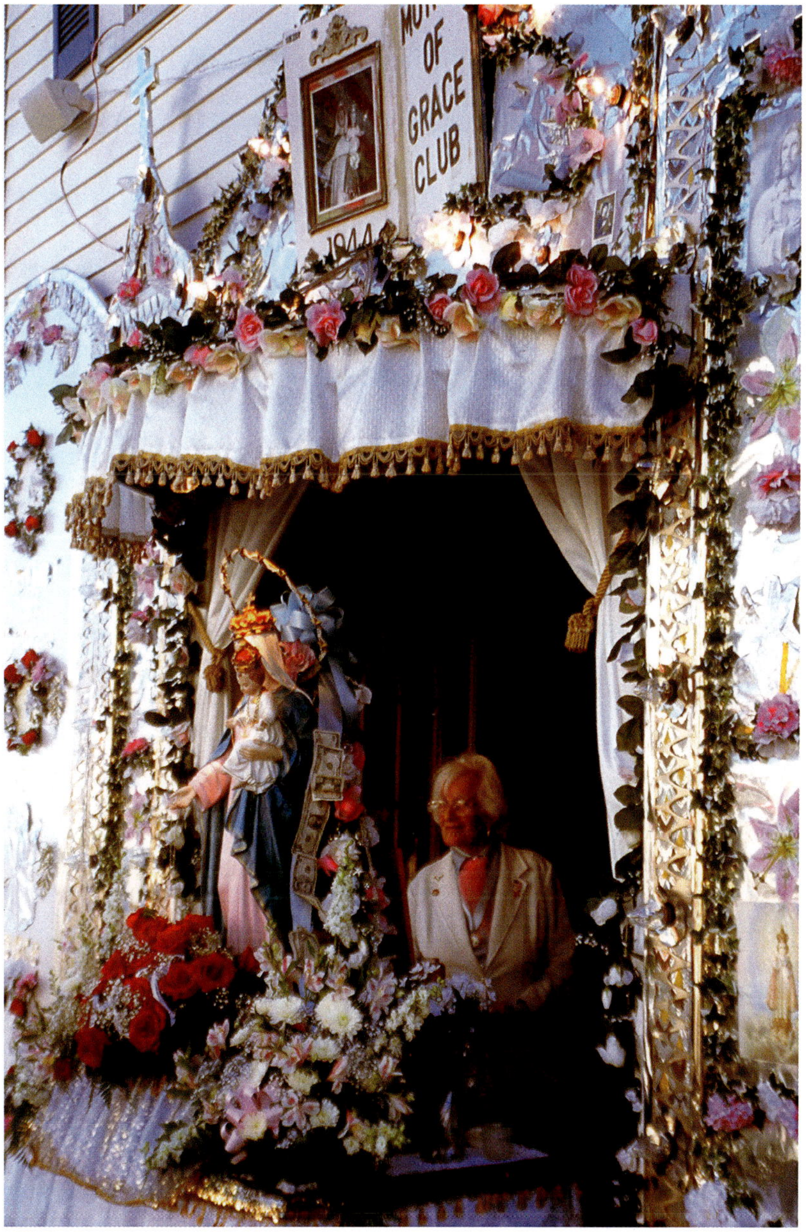
OF
GRACE
CLUB

Lanesville–The Village

The village, located in the back of the Cape, an area now known as North Gloucester, was familiar to me as a kid. We would pass through it on a Sunday drive with Uncle Homer or on a visit to Locust Grove Cemetery located just beyond the village. I liked the granite steps, walls and foundations, and the snugness of the tiny place!

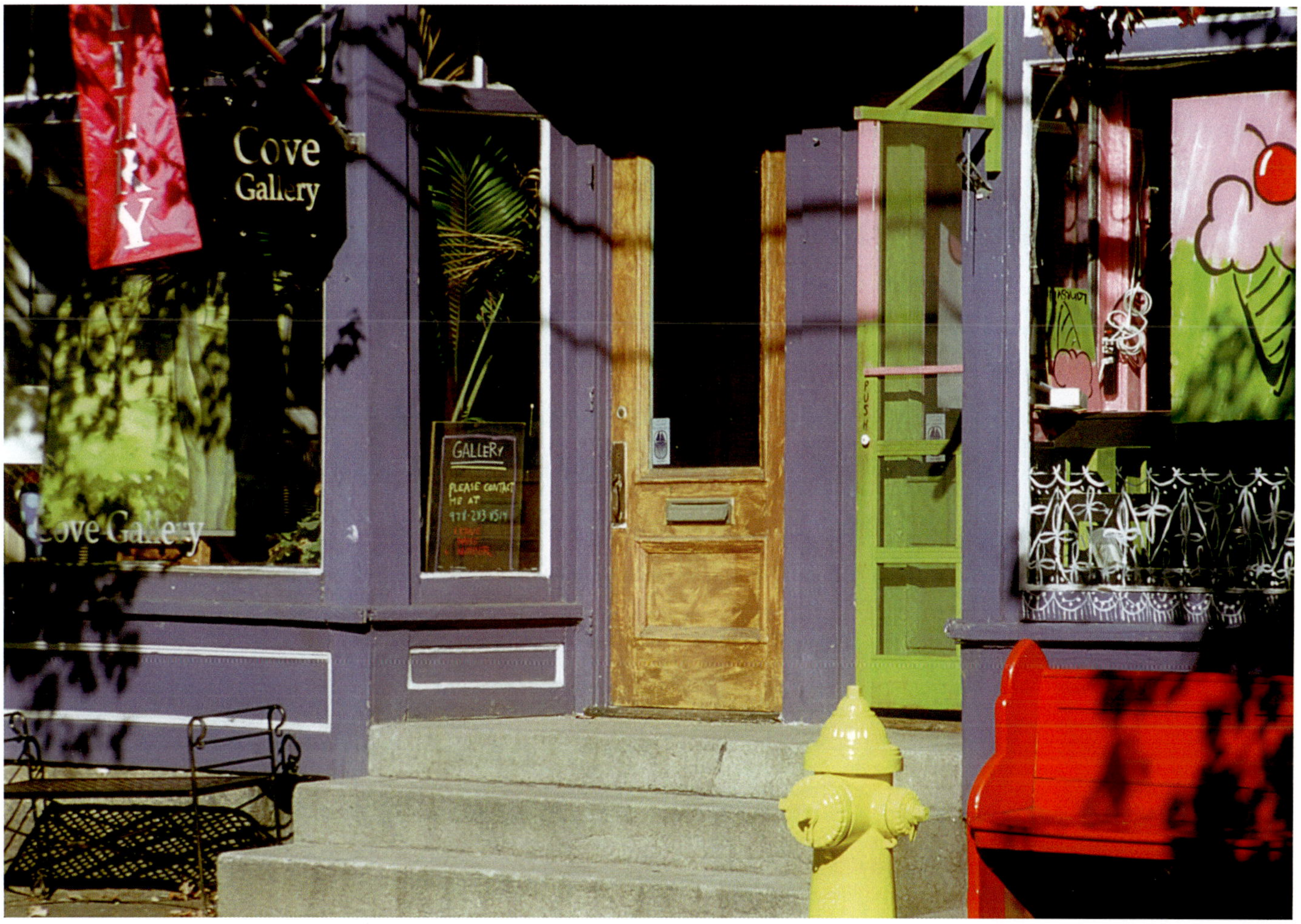
Cove
Gallery
GALLERY

Lane's Cove–Diamonds in the Water

Just beyond the village of Lanesville, (the area natives call the back of the Cape), if you take a sharp left off Route 127, you'll be facing Lane's Cove, a tiny harbor sheltered by a massive granite breakwater. It's a great place for lobstermen, local people and artists. But I often think it might not be a town landing now and a place available to all if my Dad, a city councilor for 16 years, hadn't helped to protect the cove twice during the '60s. The first time, a group of swordfishermen tried to change particular boundaries in the cove which would have prevented local fishermen from using the area. The Lanesville protectors fought that off. The second time, Boston University tried to buy the cove, intending to make it private. But my Dad, along with a group of Lanesville people, persuaded the city of Gloucester to buy the cove in 1970.

When I'm in the cove, I may be sitting on a lobster pot while I study the seaweed swirling in and out among the rocks. I may be watching a lobsterman as he slowly enters the harbor. But always, in the back of my mind, I'm thinking of the people of Lanesville and of my Dad, too, who joined forces to keep this beautiful cove public.

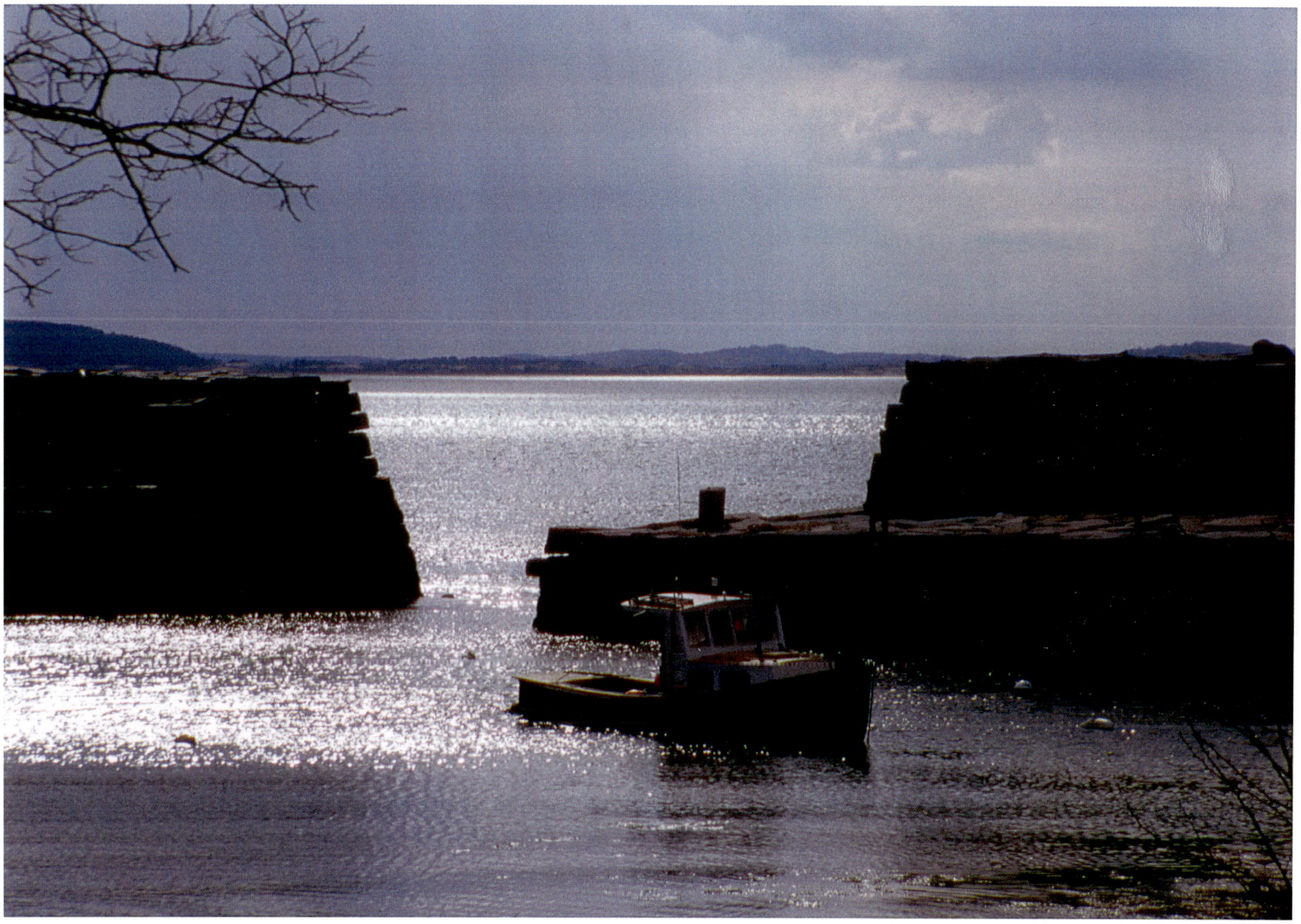

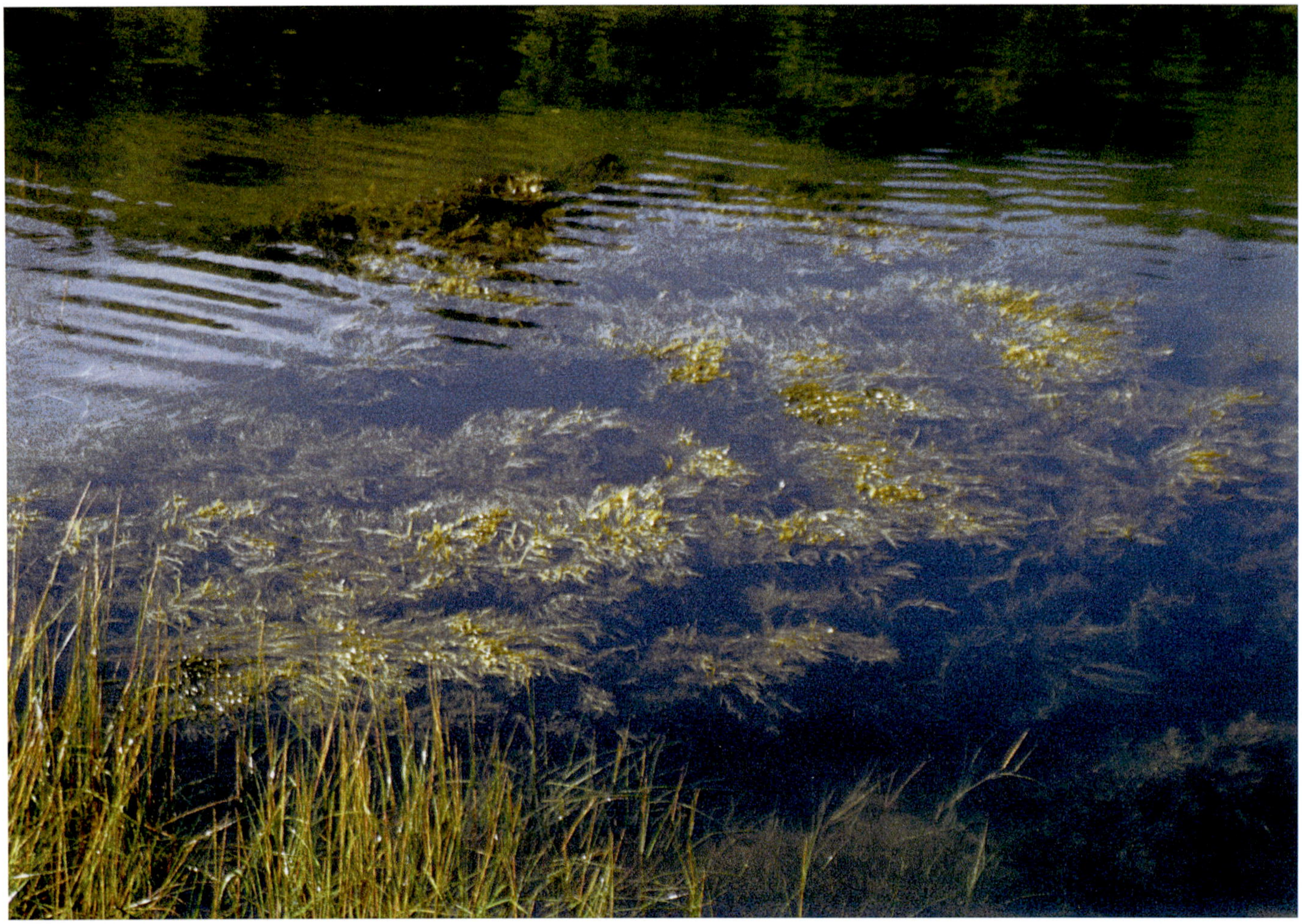

Seaweed in Lane's Cove

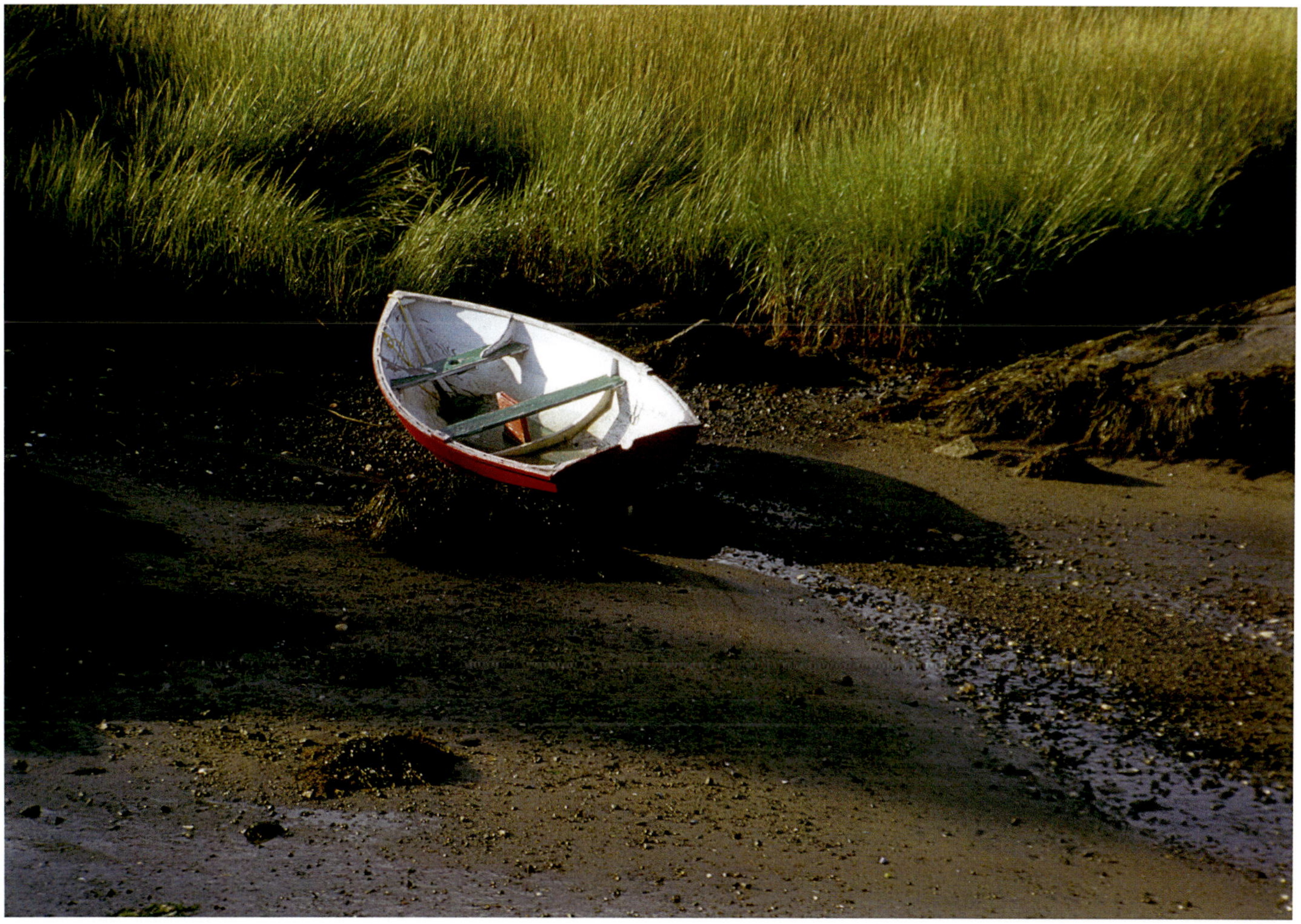

Low Tide in Lane's Cove

Sources

City of Gloucester Council. *Council Meeting Records, 1960, 1962, 1969, 1970.* Gloucester, MA.

Copeland, Melvin T., and Elliot C. Rogers. *The Saga of Cape Ann*. Freeport, Maine: Bond Wheelwright Co., 1960.

Garland, Joseph E. *The Gloucester Guide: A Stroll through Place and Time.* Charleston: History Press, 2004.

Hale, Judson D., ed. *The Old Farmer's Almanac.* 6 vols. Dublin, NH: Yankee, 2004–2009.

Patch, Isaac. *Growing Up in Gloucester*. Gloucester, MA: Curious Traveller Press, 2004.

Polk's Gloucester (Essex County, Mass.) City Directory, including Rockport. Vol. 1941–42. Boston: R.L. Polk Co., n.d.

Wright, John Hardy. *Images of America: Gloucester and Rockport.* Charleston: Arcadia, 2000.

Acknowledgments

Thank you to so very many people, including the following:

The people of Gloucester who have befriended me and cheered me on!

My children, Anne True for proofreading, Martha Frost for typing and Ben Frost for critiquing the photographs and for taking the author photograph.

Family members for answering questions and helping with history and details.

Friends for believing in me.

Jennifer Ray for editing the text.

Judith Arisman for designing and typesetting the book.

Ian Churchill for printing the mock up and for editing the photographs.

Webster Bull, publisher, for suggestions.

Bob Deschene and Joshua Morrissette for technical assistance.

Fred and Stephanie Buck of the Cape Ann Museum for locating and printing the 1947 Lucas map used in the book. The Cape Ann Savings Bank for permission to photograph the wharf scene. The Sawyer Free Library for permission to photograph the stacks.

Caylee DaSilva of Gloucester for posing for "Young Girl with Pomegranate."

Hortense L. Harris, my English teacher at Gloucester High School, for teaching me the fundamentals of writing.

All of my teachers, including Joyce Tenneson, at the Maine Media Center, Rockport, Maine.

And finally to my late husband, Dave, for always encouraging me to do what I wanted to do!

The text of this book was set in Adobe Garamond typeface. Claude Garamond [c.1480–1561] influenced type across France and Europe with his roman types. His letterforms are known for their fluidity and consistency. The digital Adobe Garamond typeface is the design of Robert Slimbach.